PEACE
BE STILL

Prayers of Intercession;
What Do You Do When Life Falls Apart?

Marcia Meikle-Naughton

authorHOUSE®

AuthorHouse™
1663 Liberty Drive
Bloomington, IN 47403
www.authorhouse.com
Phone: 1 (800) 839-8640

Published by AuthorHouse 04/22/2016

ISBN: 978-1-5049-8366-2 (sc)
ISBN: 978-1-5049-8365-5 (e)

Library of Congress Control Number: 2016903678

Print information available on the last page.

This book is printed on acid-free paper.

Scripture quotations marked NIV are taken from the Holy Bible, New International
Version®. NIV®. Copyright © 1973, 1978, 1984 by International Bible
Society. Used by permission of Zondervan. All rights reserved. [Biblica

Scripture quotations marked KJV are from the Holy Bible, King James Version
(Authorized Version). First published in 1611. Quoted from the KJV Classic
Reference Bible, Copyright © 1983 by The Zondervan Corporation.

Scripture quotations marked TLB are taken from The Living Bible
copyright © 1971. Used by permission of Tyndale House Publishers,
Inc., Carol Stream, Illinois 60188. All rights reserved.

INTRODUCTION

Peace Be Still is composed of targeted prayers birthed by the Holy Spirit. What do you do when life falls apart? How do you cope when your world as you know it disintegrates? How can you connect in a marriage when your past has left you emotionally crippled? Where do you turn when hell breaks loose behind closed doors? Who decides when to say "game over"? Who has time or wants to invest in a dysfunctional unhealthy marriage?

Feelings, and emotions, tossed on every side, life filled with anxiety, doubt and no peace — a life in turmoil; a marriage going through transition or, birthing pains. In most cases, God will use the very thing that blesses your life to cause you the most pain. Persistence, patience, diligence and obedience are the key ingredients in a recipe for deliverance and restoration. A deeper appreciation and thankfulness to God who has blessed you with a loving and kind spouse. Although none of these wonderful traits is evident, what you believe and act upon is manifesting in your spouse daily in the name of Jesus. God is in the details and nothing is impossible or too far-gone for God. The bible says clearly marriage is a covenant relationship and God instituted marriage. The average person not knowing that God is in the detail will flippantly say, I made a mistake, this is not working out for me and clearly, by his behavior and action this is not the spouse for me - I want out! Big mistake, keep pushing.

The selfish and self- centered spouse wants instant gratification, a ready- made marriage or relationship. There is no investment, nothing to put out, only expecting to receive what was not invested in the planting season. In such a case, one spouse is putting in all the work to keep the other spouse solvent. The sacrifice being, one party must shoulder the responsibility of a dysfunctional marriage, putting up with unheard of behavior, until the spouse has grown up spiritually and mentally to handle and take his rightful place in the marriage; not many people are willing to wait for an immature spouse to grow up!

How do you expect to reap when the initial investment was zero from the perspective of emotional investment, and time investment? If there was no planting of seeds, there will not be a harvest; in other words, a bankrupt marriage and relationship is net return on a zero investment.

The same in life as with any financial investment, you must invest, put a portion aside for a season for it to grow. Tend to the investment and guard against parasites that will come to eat the investment. It is not profitable to make an investment today and dig up the investment the next day. There was not enough time to compound interest on the investment; however if this investment was left for some time, there would be a guaranteed increase. Therefore, it is in the natural so it is in the spiritual. A marriage is two people coming together in faith and becoming one; each investing himself in the other. Time yields fruit and it outweighs the initial first investment in the relationship and marriage for the long term.

I can say with a level of confidence that if neither spouse is willing to trust God in the details of the marriage, and shape the attitude and focus towards each other in the marriage; the marriage will not last. Until both parties are willing to seek God to shape their character, shape their way of seeing the marriage, shape the way they appreciate each other in the marriage and bringing something new to the marriage in terms of experience and understanding, each willing to give of self and put selfishness behind, the marriage will not last.

I am of the mind that sex is the fringe benefit of a marriage, the cherry on top as a turn of phrase. Sex is not the all-in-all of the marriage. Sexual relations is important to both parties in the marriage union however sex in not the key factor in a marriage. If the sole purpose of this marriage is sexual relations and not communications, trust, and security, this marriage in time is also destined for internal implosion. Sex becomes a mechanical process over time with each partner set-up to start looking outside the marriage for attention and stimulation. In most cases, the weaker partner will be lured away, and drawn away by selfish desires.

Extricating oneself from a bad marriage is expensive and painful; emotional hurt, pain, disillusionment and most precious of all the loss of time and loss of trust. Included are promises made that were unfulfilled. If the marriage was extensive and children are involved the devastation travels to the next generation. From a financial perspective, the breaking up of a home and life is a loss all round!

Therefore with this note of caution: stepping into the union of marriage is not a trial or a test run; it is for real the first time around. Both parties must be fully invested in the marriage relationship.

I believe God answers sincere prayers. The spouse willing to do his part for the sake of the commitment and trust God will win each time. The word of God gives us many promises and Joel 2:25-26; speaks of total restoration. Supernatural transformation takes place in the heart, mind and spirit with the outworking in the flesh. Jesus is the way to total restoration; no situation is impossible, no marriage or relationship is too far-gone that God cannot transform and bring about a new beginning. All things are possible to those who believe.

Let us look at an invisible variable that you would not consider; there is an unseen enemy. This enemy travels in time from generation to generation; this enemy studies life patterns, habits, attitudes, relationships, like etc., every aspect of human life is closely studied and planned. The enemy is the devil and his fallen angels.

Spiritual warfare is real and it is taking place second by second minute by minute hour-by-hour, day by day year in and year out; the enemy is not quitting his fight for your life and your soul. This unseen battle is taking place around you a world that is more dangerous than what you can see with your natural eyes. It is no longer you walking around in a happy home; it is the enemies you face daily; demonic spirits are operating around your home, and setting traps on every side; traps set to destabilize a happy home.

Peace be Still is written for the Christian man and woman willing to go all the way to save his/her relationship in the name of Jesus; the Christian who exercises boldness and spiritual authority in prayer under pressure.

Peace be Still is composed of targeted net breaking, dismantling, paralyzing, and demolishing prayers. The enemies of our families are demonic forces, unclean spirits, demons, principalities, powers and rulers in the spiritual realm. These enemies use family members, children, husbands and wives to fight against each other. The spirits bring destruction to steal and to kill a family through alienation, separation and untimely divorce. In other words, ensuing God's plan for the family is aborted permanently. The manifestations of the working of the enemy include arguments, fights, anger, fear, hate, distrust, betrayal, manipulation, deception and separation. The demonic spirits will use any means necessary to tear down and destroy a family. Spirits will use people, places and things to bring about destruction. The demonic spirits have intelligence and study the person and the environment and will use any weakness in the person and the family as a place to gain a foothold. The enemy knows the family line intimately, through years of study and knowledge taken from the demonic realm. These spirits are without bodies; disembodied beings walking around seeking a host to inhabit and attaching themselves to an individual and through that person and controlling his/her actions etc. (You may ask, how do the spirits come in, what attracts them? How do we know we are not walking around with one of these spirits)?

The devil or Satan is not intimidated by weak faithless prayers; he is afraid of the faith filled Christian bombarding the 2nd heaven with fire applying the word of God as a weapon. The enemy is afraid of the faith-filled believer who prays in faith and authority. Faith activates the move of God!

Christians who are saved and love the Lord have this spiritual authority to bind and cast out demons. Peace be Still focuses on targeting the wickedness in the 2nd heaven, the place of demonic activity. Pulling down, paralyzing, casting down and destroying the work of demons and principalities operating in homes, communities, cities and nations.

Therefore, *Peace be Still* is written for the warrior Christian in the faith of Gideon. Warriors in our homes protecting and keeping what God has blessed us to attain and by guarding and maintaining a hedge of protection around our families and possessions and subsequently sustaining love, peace, happiness, tranquility, prosperity, wealth in our homes and families. Ascertaining and praying for communities, cities and nation. Pray against the confederacy of the enemy.

Peace be Still comes against the Spirit of Turmoil that comes in the form of destruction, the spirit of basilisk going into every form or place of the Christian's life. A good example is a man and woman in a covenant relationship experiencing sudden unexpected attacks in their relationship. Attacks which come in all forms and seeping into: family, health and finances. In other words, attacks that are unexpected and unknown changing and dismantling a relationship. For example – a loving marriage suddenly under severe demonic attack. (Now: Warfare is not only necessary and required to save this marriage from the enemy of the divorce spirit is a must at all cost! The spirits that expect to gain a foothold in the marriage are not giving up but fighting day and night, trying to wear down your faith to give up.

Bewitchment is sent against the marriage to confuse and dislocate. Spirits of Witchcraft and Sorcery and Divination to control, manipulate and harass. Cohort spirits come along to bring in confusion and turmoil the end result marriage destruction. The arsenal to the Christian is warfare on his/her knees! This is the time to take off l "all" restraints in prayer and go into full battle gear armored according to Ephesian 6:10-17. Your success is to win back and restore your marriage and place it completely under the blood covering of Jesus Christ.

The word says to pray with all types of prayers armed with the word of God. This is a military strategy and therefore not for the faint hearted. The enemy of our soul, our marriage and relationship is trespassing on consecrated territory! The devil's key purpose is to kill, steal and destroy the marriage and relationship. The Lord came to give life and life more abundantly; our counter attack is to annihilate and mortally wound the enemy. As we go into warfare for our relationships and families the end result permanent destruction of the enemy in all areas. The goal is to secure families, possessions and our peace of mind.

"... not by might nor by power, but by my spirit saith the Lord of host." (Zech 4:6)

<u>Caution</u>: The <u>unsaved</u> man/woman is not given this authority. Jesus is not Lord in the life of the unsaved. The authority to war in Jesus name is the right and privilege given to the Christian at the cross.

Satan is lord to the unsaved; self is the ruler in Satan's kingdom.

All things are possible to those who believe.

This book on prayers is the process God used to develop my character to release, hurt and pain through his love and the ministry of forgiveness. The act of forgiveness birthed ministry, "All things work together for good to those who love God and are called according to his purpose." (Romans 8:28). I developed a closer walk with Jesus and know there is power in the name; there is great power in forgiveness; not lip service but willing to ask God for help to release people who have tried to devastate your life through their behavior and actions.

Prayer is the foundation of our Christian faith and is the building block that strengthens our walk each day. Prayer calms the pressure and gives us peace. We become warriors in the spirit when we submit in prayer and fasting. We gain access to power through obedience and reading the word of God. The Word of God is life breathe and therefore the word of God is the answer to any problem.

The first criteria in this walk of faith is Salvation; you must be willing to accept and confess Jesus Christ as your Lord and Savior. Pray Salvation over yourself according to (Roman 10:9)

- Ask for forgiveness and forgive others
- Repent of known and unknown sins
- Spend time in the word of God.
- Build up your prayer life
- Make daily confessions of Faith in God

- Pray and speak blessings over marriage, family and relationships, health and finances
- Activate your Faith daily
- Exercise authority in Prayer

(Nuggets for the soul: victory in Jesus name)

Thank you my father, as the reader opens the book and begin to activate his/her faith and applies your word; let the power of God flow through the pages in Jesus name. Let the resurrection power of Jesus Christ manifest in his/her life to bring forth the change they believe to see in Jesus name. My father, fill him/her with the spiritual authority that comes from your word - power to tread on snakes and scorpions, and every power of the enemy and nothing shall by any means hurt them in the name of Jesus. (Luke 10:19)

Let this be a new season in the life of this person, seeking your face and not your hand in the name of Jesus. Let the supernatural power begin to manifest in his/her life as they step out in faith and use your word as a hammer in the spiritual realm. Let the Holy Spirit release supernatural power as the word of God is spoken through these prayers. Bless their marriages, bless their families and bless their relationships in the name of Jesus Amen.

"My peace I leave with you, my peace I give you". (John 14:27)

FOREWORD

Father God in the name of Jesus, I give you all honor and praise that you have anointed me to write and pray your word over marriages and relationships in the name of Jesus. I thank you, my father. You have made me pregnant with a precious gift. I am walking in the pathway of a woman growing with new life daily, to speak and write your words in Jesus name.

As I approach childbirth, guide my steps with loving kindness and tender mercies so the enemy cannot prematurely destroy the seed you have implanted in me. Let the pregnancy come to full term, in the name of Jesus. Father God in the name of Jesus, as the labor pains come forth, give me strength to fight to endure the attacks of the enemy.

Father you are my comfort, my peace and my joy so therefore I submit my life, my heart to you this day in the name of Jesus. I am your servant, and I am walking in the pathway you have revealed to me. My heart is fixed and I am allowing you to lead and guide me daily in obedience to you. I plead the blood of Jesus over my life and those connected to me in the name of Jesus. Father God destroy and paralyze every spirit that is not like you that will try to come against your word and your work in the name of Jesus. Let the life of every believer seeking change in his or her marriage and relationships be transformed by the power of Jesus Christ. "Stand therefore, having girded your waist with truth, having put on the breastplate of righteousness, and having shod your feet with the preparation of the gospel of peace; above all, taking the shield of faith with which you will be able to quench all the fiery darts of the wicked one." (Ephesians 6: 14-16)

"Have respect therefore to the prayer of thy servant, and to his supplication, O LORD my God, to hearken unto the cry and the prayer which thy servant prayeth before thee." (2 Chronicles 6:19)

SPECIAL ACKNOWLEDGMENTS

I want to give praise and honor to the Lord Jesus Christ for life, grace and blessings. My father you are worthy of all the praise and honor at all times. I want to acknowledge the Holy Spirit my constant companion. Thank you Holy Spirit. Thank you for the times when I could not see or hear. Thank you for the shield of protection you placed on me; thank you for your loving kindness and tender mercies towards me. I stand naked and unashamed before you my Lord; I came a long way to say that you shielded me from the plan of the enemy to destroy my life; I am still here fighting the good fight of faith. I am your servant, I cover myself in the blood of Jesus; I submit my life into your hands in the name of Jesus.

I want to express deep appreciation and thankfulness for the teaching I receive at the Temple of Restoration on a weekly basis. Bishop Angelo Barbosa my Pastor is a man called and anointed by God. I learned to activate and speak faith into my life and affairs through the teaching I received. Bishop Barbosa is my example of a man walking in faith and manifesting the glory of God in his life. Listening to his testimonies has brought my faith to a new level in the manifestation and the power of God. Bishop Barbosa taught me by example to walk in authority and to speak the word of God in faith.

I would also like to thank all the pastors at The Temple of Restoration and give a special acknowledgement to Pastor Rosalie for counseling and praying with me. I want to also give special thanks to Pastor John for encouraging me to pray for my family and fight for my marriage. I owe a special thanks to all the Pastors at TTOR (Pastor Junior, Ms. Liz. Pastor Raul) thank you for the many prayers!

I would also like to thank Pastor AR Bernard from Christian Cultural Center for foundational teachings on the word of God. I can proudly say as a past member of CCC for the past 14 years; Pastor Bernard taught the word of God and has blessed me to move forward in the name of Jesus.

I want to give special thanks to the Derek Prince Ministries. Derek Prince, an amazing teacher of the Scriptures passed away many years ago; however, his teaching is still alive online. I thank God for his focus and deep dive into the word of God to bring out such deep revelation. Derek Prince built my faith in marriage and showed me the value of marriage and understanding roles for husbands and wives. This man of God transformed my thinking on marriage. He emphasized that marriage is a covenant and not so much about all the things we glorify when getting married, but know that God brings a man and woman together for his purpose and plan. Therefore, I held this close to my heart as I walked in the place of testing.

I also want to express a special thank you to a blessed group of women – the "Women on the Wall" Prayer Group. This amazing group of women meet to pray each day at 5:00am to pray for families and our nations. I would also like to thank the Thursday 8:00pm Prayer group – "Women Praying for our Men". God sowed the seed into my spirit through the ministry of my sister Mary Floyd who is an awesome woman with a vision from God. Mary and I spoke and God unleased the vision in my spirit to support her in this vison of ministering to men. Praying for men to take their rightful place in marriages, families, communities our nation and the world.

I thank God for my daughter Brianna Chelsea Perez. The Lord blessed me with a wonderful, wise daughter. The Lord blessed me to raise her believing that nothing is impossible through faith. Today Brianna is happily married to a wonderful man of God, Ray Perez Jr.

The start of my personal ministry was the day I got married in 2014.

I had to walk through the valley of dry bones according to Ezekiel 37:1-14, I had to call the dry bones back to life and trust God to bring forth restoration, healing of mind, heart and spirit. God kept me in peace as I kept my heart and mind on him. My faith had to be raised to a new level during the season of testing; God gave me a new start and a new life. Faith moves mountains.

"Now faith is the substance of things hoped for the evidence of thing not seen." Hebrew 11:1

Marcia Meikle-Naughton (aka: Lady Peace MN)

Prayer Content

- Prayer against the Spirit of Bewitchment
- Prayer against Witchcraft/ and Ungodly Prayers
- Marriage and Relationships
- Prayer for a God Chosen Wife
- Deliverance Prayer – Husband's Responsibility
- Deliverance Prayer for Men
- Deliverance Prayer Sons and Brothers
- Prayer against the Spirit of Turmoil and the Spirit of Confusion
- Prayer against Deception and Manipulation
- Prayers against Marital Strongholds/Oppression
- Prayers against Adultery/Infidelity/Sexual Sins
- Prayers against Marital Destruction
- Prayer Marriage (Mess-up) Cleanup
- Prayer against: Arrested Development Syndrome (Dyslexia and ADHD)
- Prayer against Behavioral Disorders (Sociopath Behaviors)
- Prayer against Behavioral Disorders (Bi-Polar and Manic Depressant Behavior)

- Prayer against Addictive Spirits (Sexual Addictions, Drug Addictions)
- I will bring Health and Cure
- Prayer against Suicide and Premature Death
- Prayer against: The Demon Anger (Murder, Violence and Death)
- Prayer against Unrepentant Enemies
- Prayer to Release the Promise of God
- Prayer for Career and Job Release
- Prayer against Backlash and Retaliation

Psalms 23: The Lord is my shepherd I shall not want…

Psalms 91: He who dwells in the secret place of the most high…

Ephesians 6: 10- 17 (Spiritual Armor)

Prayer against the Spirit of Bewitchment

Father God in the name of Jesus, I come to you asking for forgiveness, sins known and unknown, cleanse my heart mind, will and emotions in Jesus name.

> In the name of Jesus, 1 plead the blood of Jesus over my mind, body, soul and spirit. I plead the blood of Jesus over my family and those closely connect to me. I plead the blood of Jesus over my possessions, my finances and my home in the name of Jesus.
>
> In the name of Jesus, I bind the spirits of rebellion," For rebellion *is as* the sin of witchcraft, and stubbornness *is as* iniquity and idolatry... (I Samuel 15:23).
>
> In the name of Jesus, I bind the spirit of disobedience. "Let no man deceive you with vain words: for because of these things cometh the wrath of God upon the children of disobedience." (Ephesian 5:6)
>
> In the name of Jesus, I bind the spirit of unbelief: So we see that they could not enter in because of unbelief. (Hebrew 3:19)
>
> Father God in the name of Jesus, I send the fire of God against the operation of witchcraft in the

name of Jesus. "And I will cut off witchcrafts out of thine hand; and thou shalt have no *more* soothsayers" (Micah 5:12)

Regard not them that have familiar spirits, neither seek after wizards, to be defiled by them: I [am] the LORD your God. (Leviticus 19:31).

I plead the blood of Jesus against the spirits of Jezebel and Ahab. "And of Jezebel also spake the LORD, saying, the dogs shall eat Jezebel by the wall of Jezreel." (I Kings 21:23)." But there was none like unto Ahab, which did sell himself to work wickedness in the sight of the LORD, whom Jezebel his wife stirred up." (Kings 21:25)

I bind paralyze and destroy the spirits of Jezebel and Ahab in my life and my family in the name of Jesus.

I bind the spirit of sorcery. "But there was a certain man, called Simon, which before time in the same city used sorcery, and bewitched the people of Samaria, giving out that himself was some great one". (Acts 8:9)

I bind the demon spirit of Leviathan. "In that day the LORD with his sore and great and strong sword shall punish leviathan the piercing serpent, even leviathan that crooked serpent; and he shall slay the dragon that [is] in the sea." (Isiah 27:1) "Or a charmer, or a consulter with familiar spirits, or a wizard, or a necromancer." (Deuteronomy 18:11)

I bind the spirit of divination. "For the king of Babylon stood at the parting of the way, at the head of the two ways, to use divination: he made *his* arrows bright, he consulted with images, he looked in the liver". (Ezekiel 21:21)

I bind the spirit of the occult. "And when they shall say unto you, Seek unto them that have familiar spirits, and unto wizards that peep, and that mutter: should not a people seek unto their God for the living to the dead? (Isiah 8:19)

I bind the spirit of deception in Jesus name.

I bind the lying spirit in Jesus name. "Now therefore, behold, the LORD hath put a lying spirit in the mouth of all these thy prophets, and the LORD hath spoken evil concerning thee. "(Kings 22:23)

I bind controlling spirit in Jesus name. "But the Spirit of the LORD departed from Saul, and an evil spirit from the LORD troubled him". (1 Samuel 16:14)

I bind the spirit of rejection in Jesus name. "Think not that I am come to send peace on earth: I came not to send peace, but a sword". (Matt 10:34)

I bind manipulating spirits in the name of Jesus. "And no marvel; for Satan himself is transformed into an angel of light". (2 Corinthians 11:14)

I bind the spirit of slavery in the name of Jesus. **"While they promise them liberty, they themselves are the servants of corruption: for of whom a man is overcome, of the same is he brought in bondage". 2 Peter 2:19)**

I bind intimidation spirits in the name of Jesus. "Be sober, be vigilant; because your adversary the devil, as a roaring lion, walketh about, seeking whom he may devour." (1 Peter 5:8)

I bind the spirit of legion in Jesus name." And Jesus asked him, saying, what is thy name? And he said, Legion: because many devils were entered into him." Luke 8:30

I bind the spirit of idolatry in Jesus name. "Mortify therefore your members which are upon the earth; fornication, uncleanness, inordinate affection, evil concupiscence, and covetousness, which is idolatry". (Colossian 3:5)

I bind the spirits of jealousy in Jesus name. "For jealousy [is] the rage of a man: therefore he will not spare in the day of vengeance." (Proverbs 6:34.

I bind the spirit of envy in Jesus name. "Envy thou not the oppressor, and choose none of his ways." (Proverbs3:31)

I bind the degenerative spirit in the name of Jesus.

I bind mind-controlling spirits in the name of Jesus.

I bind the spirits of grudge and malice in the name of Jesus

I bind the spirit of hatred and covetous in Jesus name.

I bind the confused spirit in the name of Jesus.

I bind the spiritual and religious spirits in Jesus name.

1 bind the spirit of isolation in Jesus name.

I bind the spirits of captivity and entanglement in Jesus name.

1 bind soul ties and inordinate affection with unfriendly friends and enemies in the name of Jesus,

I bind the spirit of enchantment." Stand now with thine enchantments, and with the multitude of thy sorceries, wherein thou hast labored from thy youth; if so be thou shalt be able to profit, if so be thou mayest prevail." (Isiah 47:12)

I bind false religions in the name of Jesus

I bind the spirit of heresy

I bind the spirit of hypocrisy

1 bind the spirit of fear in Jesus name.

I bind the spirit of fornication and adultery in the name of Jesus

I bind the spirt of lust in the name of Jesus

I bind the charismatic snake spirit in the name of Jesus

1 bind the spirit of slumber in Jesus name.

1 bind the spirit of confusion in Jesus name.

1 bind loss of identity in Jesus name.

1 bind the spirit of infirmity (sickness, disease, pestilence, pain and aches) in the name of Jesus.

1 bind the spirit of heaviness in Jesus name.

1 bind the spirit of depression and oppression in Jesus name.

I bind the spirit of rejection in the name of Jesus

1 bind prophetic divination in Jesus name.

1 bind assignment demons whose purpose is to entice, pressure enslave, torment, compel and defile, harass and deceive; I destroy them to the root in the name of Jesus.

1 bind the spirit of restlessness in Jesus name.

1 bind the spirit of slumber in Jesus name.

1 bind a wounded spirit which came through hurt, fear and pride.

1 bind, cancel and destroy the spirit of bewitchment, enchantment, and black arts and destroy its power forever over my life and the lives of my family in Jesus name.

1 bind the python spirit, the serpentine spirit, whose purpose is to squeeze out my prayer life and derail my purpose. I destroy you today by the blood of Jesus, in Jesus name.

I bind the marine spirit in the name of Jesus.

1 break witchcraft dark influence in Jesus name.

1 break witchcraft powers in Jesus name.

In the name of Jesus, 1 renounce witchcraft, divination, and sorcery in Jesus name. Father if there was an opening a door through horoscopes, Ouija boards or other occult means, 1 close the door forever by the blood of Jesus.

1 renounce spirits of enchantments in the name of Jesus.

1 renounce all spirits that is not the Holy Spirit from my life and the life of my family members in the name of Jesus.

1 destroy its roots and cast out it out by the blood of Jesus in Jesus name.

"Beloved, believe not every spirit, but try the spirits whether they are of God: because many false prophets are gone out into the world." (1 John 4:1-3)

Howbeit when he, the Spirit of truth, is come, he will guide you into all truth: for he shall not speak of himself; but whatsoever he shall hear, [that] shall he speak: and he will shew you things to come. (John 16:13)

Father God in the name of Jesus, today 1 surrender my life completely to you and ask you Lord; fill every vacancy with the Holy Spirit in the name of Jesus. In the name of Jesus, 1 cancel the spirit of bewitchment over my life first and my family members, finances, prosperity, health employment – job, place of work, business, and church.

1 declare and decree today, financial increase, an outpouring of blessing is finding me and my generations for a 1000 years in the name of Jesus. Father God 1 thank you for total restoration of my life, my family, possessions, finances, job, businesses, and profession in name of Jesus. 1 seal this prayer with the blood of Jesus a prayer and blessing that cannot be reversed.

Wealth and riches is my house in my generation. The blessings of the Lord makes riche and he adds no sorrow. (Amen)

Deuteronomy 18:10-14; Jeremiah 29:11, Leviticus 19:31, Isiah 8:19, 2 Kings 21:6, Leviticus 20: 6, 27, Nahum 3:4, Ezekiel 13: 18, 20, Isiah 44:25, Jeremiah 9: 2-6, Philippians 6: 23

Galatians 3:10, Galatians 5:1 – 26, I Chronicles 10: 13 – 14, I Kings 16- 30-31; 11Kings 18, Galatians 5:20, Revelations 21:8

The Lord will bless his people with peace (Psalms 29:11)

Prayer against Witchcraft and Ungodly Covenant Prayers

Father God in the name of Jesus, I praise and glorify you as God. I thank you for your amazing grace in Jesus name. Thank you for the power that is given to me through your word. In your word my Lord" you have given unto me power to trample on snakes and scorpions and over all power of the enemy and nothing can by any means hurt me," in Jesus name. (Luke 10:19)

Lord I ask for forgiveness for any sin in my life, sins of omission and sins of commission. I repent of the sin of unforgiveness, unbelief and rebellion in the name of Jesus.

I ask for forgiveness for sins of my generations going back 1000 years in the name of Jesus. Lord if my family had an ungodly covenant with witchcraft or ungodly covenant, I break it now by the blood of Jesus in the name of Jesus.

Father God in the name of Jesus I bind the power of **witchcraft** "And I will cut off witchcraft out of thine hand; and thou shalt have no *more* soothsayers." (Micah 5:2) "For rebellion *is as* the sin of witchcraft, and stubbornness *is as* iniquity and idolatry.".(1 Samuel 15:23)

>I bind sorcery in my life and my family in the name of Jesus. "And the soul that turneth after such as have familiar spirits, and after wizards, to go a whoring after them, I will even set my face against that soul, and will cut him off from among his people." (Leviticus 20:6) I bind the demon Leviathan and marine spirits in Jesus name, powers unleashed in my generation through ungodly covenants of my ancestors I break right now. I bind the traveling spirits and the spirit of turmoil "From whence [come] wars and fighting's among you? [come they] not hence, [even] of your lusts that war in your members "(James 4:1), in the Jesus name. I bind the spirit of fantasy. I bind the spirit of grief/guilt/shame and condemnation in the name of Jesus. I bind the spirit of grudge." Grudge not one against another, brethren, lest ye be condemned: behold, the judge standeth before the door." (James 5:9)

I bind malice. "Brethren, be not children in understanding: howbeit in malice be ye children, but in understanding be men." (I Corinthians 14:20)

I bind covetousness. "But thine eyes and thine heart *are* not but for thy covetousness, and for to shed innocent blood, and for oppression, and for violence, to do *it*." (Jeremiah 22:17)

I bind the spirit of mind control and mind destruction in the name of Jesus. "And be not conformed to this world: but be ye transformed by the renewing of your mind, that ye may prove what [is] that good, and acceptable, and perfect, will of God (Romans 12:2). I bind the spirit of parasite in the name of Jesus. Where their worm dieth not, and the fire is not quenched. (Mark 9:38)

By the blood of Jesus, I cancel and destroy the works of trafficking demonic spirits. "Wherefore thus saith the Lord GOD; Behold, I am against your pillows, wherewith ye there hunt the souls to make [them] fly, and I will tear them from your arms, and will let the souls go, [even] the souls that ye hunt to make [them] fly."(Ezekiel 13:20) operating on astral assignments in Jesus name. I come against every dominion and domination and assignment over my life and life of my family and community in the name of Jesus. By the blood of Jesus, I bind witchcraft psychic power and mind control in the name of Jesus. I break every cord, and line in the name of Jesus name. I bind psychic visions, charms and veil by the blood of Jesus.

My Lord "the weapons of our warfare are not carnal but mighty to the pulling down of strongholds," in the name of Jesus. (11 Corinthians 10:4)

By the blood of Jesus every unclean spirit "For he said unto him, Come out of the man, THOU unclean spirit." (Mark 5:8) In the name of Jesus every spirit having access and operating in my life, my family health and finances, I command you to depart right now to the pit of hell in the name of Jesus.

In the name of Jesus, I speak destruction into the camp of witchcraft, and cohort spirits in the 2nd heaven. I paralyze and cancel every confederacy and plot over my life, family and generations in the name of Jesus.

My father in the name of Jesus, reverse every curse of the enemy against my life, against the life of my family and generations for a 1000 years. Destroy the works and plan of witchcraft dark powers operating in secret. I wash myself, family and generations with the blood of Jesus. I sprinkle the blood of Jesus over my family line my generations for 1000 years and break the curse in Jesus name.

Father God, in the name of Jesus Christ of Nazareth, I seal my life, family and generations by the blood of

Jesus today. I release the blessings of the Lord over my generations for 1000 years according to Deuteronomy 28:1-14 in Jesus name. I declare and decree an open heaven, blessings, favor, prosperity, excellent health, enlarged territories is the portion of my generations for 1000 years in Jesus name. (Amen).

Psalms 18:34, Psalms 35:8, Galatians 5:20; 1 Samuel 15:23, Ezekiel 12:24, Acts 16:16, Leviticus 19:31, Isiah 8:19, Leviticus 20:27, Nahum 3:4, Galatians 5: 1-26

Deuteronomy 18:10, Ezekiel 21:21, Jeremiah 14:14, Acts 8:18, Acts 8:11, Galatians 3:1, Mark 3:30, Mark 5:8, Mark 5:2, Mark 1:26, Luke 11:24, Luke 8:29, Ephesians 2:12, Jeremiah 9:2-6, Ephesians 6: 10-20

Finally, brethren, farewell. Be perfect, be of good comfort, be of one mind, live in peace and the God of love and peace shall be with you. <u>2 Corinthians 13:11</u>

Deliverance Prayer – Marriage and Relationships

Lord 1 give you the praise, honor, and glory that you are God, the Savior over marriages. Father God you put marriages and relationships together. According to Leviticus 17:11 - your word said the life of all flesh is in the blood. Father God marriage is a covenant relationship before you Lord. Marriage is holy before you my father a union between a man and woman. Your word says a man shall leave his mother and father and shall be joined to his wife and they shall be one flesh (Matt 19: 4-6).

Father God, marriage is not a convenience; Marriage is a committed relationship before you in the name of Jesus. Included in the marriage pledge is a partnership relationship that is only broken through death "until death do us part." Father God as a covenant relationship the bond is in Jesus name and the blessings from you father is upon those who honor marriage as a covenant before you.

In the name of Jesus, my father as I come before you on behalf of our men Lord 1 lift them up to you now. I ask you lord to give them eyes to see and ears to hear in the name of Jesus. In the name of Jesus open their understanding, open their hearts, minds and spirit to the sacred holy covenant of marriage between a man and a woman.

In the name of Jesus, the enemy came in to distort marriages, to pervert marriages, I stand on the word of God and bring marriages before you between a man and woman in Jesus name.

My father, in the name of Jesus, teach men to forsake distraction, duplicity, lies, deceit and every plot of the enemy to bring in distrust and confusion. Father God direct their attention their heart, soul and spirit to the blessing you have given them in a wife a best friend, a companion, a lover in the name of Jesus.

Father God teach men submission, according to Romans 6:16, "know ye not, that to whom ye yield yourselves servants to obey, his servants ye are to whom ye obey; whether of sin unto death, or of obedience unto righteousness"? According to Ephesians 6:18: Let men continually "pray always with all prayer and supplication in the Spirit, and watching thereunto with all perseverance and supplication for all saints"; Father God teach men to take care of their homes, love their wives, financially support their home and rear their children with love and discipline in Jesus name.

In the name of Jesus, teach men to take their rightful place as the head of the household, taking on the responsibility and accountability of a family in Jesus name. Teach men responsibility for a home and family in the name of Jesus. Teach men that work is the means to keep a family financially secure in Jesus name. Teach men that to work to hold a job and take care of family is a responsibility and obligation given to the man to take care of his home in Jesus name. Teach men to remain faithful in communication to their spouses in Jesus name. According to 1 Timothy 3-5- "if a man knows not how to rule his own house he cannot do anything else for you my father in Jesus name."

Father God in the name of Jesus let not the sun go down on their anger. According James 1:19, let men be slow to speak and quick to hear in the name of Jesus.

According to Ephesian 5:22 "Wives, submit to your own husbands, as to the Lord." Father God, teach wives to submit to their own husbands in the name of Jesus. According Timothy 2:5 – "wives art to be discreet, chaste, keepers at home, good, obedient to their own husbands, that the word of God be not blasphemed." My father teach wives to support their husbands and to encourage them through their submission in Jesus name. My Father as wives submit to their husbands in love, the husband is in submission to you in Jesus name. The husband is able to walk in the role as the priest of the home in the name of Jesus. Father God in the name of Jesus through his obedience to you my father a husband will sacrifice himself for the wife's good and the sake of the marriage covenant in Jesus name.

Lord in intimacy my father, teach men to be affectionate and loving in Jesus name. Father God the marriage bed is undefiled, and 1 bind the spirit of Jezebel and Ahab, and Atahaliah in Jesus name. 1 bind the spirit of python and every serpentine spirit that try to curl around the leg or the head of the marriage relationship in the name of Jesus.

In the name of Jesus I bind witchcraft, sorcery, divination and dark forces sent against the marriage in the name of Jesus. I bind the spirits of lust, adultery, perversion, fantasies and demonic forces and principalities from the 2nd heaven in Jesus name. I crush the head of the enemy and his interference in marriage in the name of Jesus.

I plead the blood of Jesus over the marriage bed in the name of Jesus. According to Hebrews 13:4 - let married life be honored among all of you and not made unclean; for men untrue in married life will be judged by God. According to Isiah 57:17, no weapon that is formed against marriages will prosper in the name of Jesus.

Song of Solomon 8:7 -Many waters cannot quench love, neither can the floods drown it: if a man would give all the substance of his house for love, it would utterly be condemned. Father God, in the name of Jesus, release love, and passion in marriages in the name of Jesus. Let their bodies be a delight to each other in the name of Jesus. Father God, a man was created for his wife and the wife was created for the husband so therefore Father in the union of marriage let there be oneness and satisfaction in the marriage bed in the name of Jesus.

My father teach men to be great lovers to their wives, passionate and giving in the name of Jesus. Holy Spirit instruct and direct them in areas where they are weak in Jesus name. My father you are concerned about every aspect of men's lives and my father sexual relations and marital satisfaction is a central part of a marriage. Marital growth, happiness and fulfillment a right of a married couple in Jesus name. Father God 1 bind the spirit of fear and the spirit of performance anxiety over men in Jesus name. Lord 1 release the blessings and favor of the Lord over men to be great lovers to their wives and not be inhibited in sexual relations in Jesus name.

I bind the spirit of slavery in the name of Jesus

I bind the spirit of abandonment in the name of Jesus

I bind the spirit of neglect in Jesus name

I bind the spirit of emotional, physical and psychological abuse in Jesus name

I bind the spirit of separation and divorce in Jesus name

I bind the spirit of hatred/malice/jealousy in Jesus name

I bind the spirit of the strange man/ strange woman in the name of Jesus

Father God nothing is too hard for you and the most intimate details of men is important to you, so Lord 1 thank you for doing a new work in men today in Jesus name. In the name of Jesus, no illegal trespass will cross the bloodline of their marriage in Jesus name.

Lord Jesus as men build a life together in their marriages; Lord let your purpose and plans for their future be unfolded to them in Jesus name. According to 11 Corinthians 9:8 – "Lord you are able to make grace abound in marriages in the name of Jesus".

Father God in money matter, financial affairs, decisions related to money, finances, let there be transparency in Jesus name. Father God bind up double talk and lies regarding money matters in Jesus name. Let honesty and sincerity regarding money matter be the focus of the marriage in Jesus name. I bind the spirit of suspicion, manipulation and deceit related to financial matters in Jesus name. I bind the spirit of rejection in the name of Jesus.

In the name of Jesus equip men to plan and focus on the family for the short and long terms in financial affairs in the name of Jesus. In the name of Jesus give the man your financial plan for his life and money in the name of Jesus.

Father God according to Matt 19:4-6, "For this reason a man shall leave his father and mother and be joined to his wife, and the two shall become one flesh'? So then, they are no longer two but one flesh. Therefore what God has joined together, let not man separate)". What you have joined, let no man, no woman, no demon, no principality put asunder in the name of Jesus. I thank you for long life for our men;, I thank you for excellent health, strength, vigor, vitality and endurance in the name of Jesus. I declare and decree successful Christ centered fulfilled marriages, in body, soul and spirit in Jesus name. Father God 1 declare and decree marriages are heaven on earth in Jesus name. Amen, Amen.

Hebrews 13:4, Luke 20:34, 2 Corinthians 6:4, Psalms 127:1, Galatians 5:1, 2 Timothy 3: 6, Roman 12:1- 21, John 13:34, Genesis 1:27 Galatians 5:22-23, James 1:2, Ephesians 5:15, 1 Peter 3; 1-22, James 3: 3 – 12, Ephesian 6:12

———————————————————

Prayer for a God (Chosen) Wife

My father, I give you the praise today for saving my life. I rejoice in you today because through the blood of Jesus I am standing on the promises in your word. I give you the praise and honor that you loved me so much you set me apart and protected me from seen and unseen dangers in the name of Jesus.

Lord, I come with a humble request today, your word says to ask and I shall receive in Jesus name. My father, I am asking you for a godly wife, a companion, a friend and a lover. Lord a woman that I will find attractive, appealing a woman who will complete me as a man in the name of Jesus. Father God a woman who will fulfil the purpose you have put into me and for us to grow into the oneness of a covenant relationship as man and wife.

Lord I am asking you for a wife who will be my soul mate and the mother of our children. "Whoso findeth a wife findeth a good thing, and obtained favour of the LORD." (Proverbs 18:22)

"Nevertheless let every one of you in particular so love his wife even as himself; and the wife *see* that she reverence *her* husband." Lord as I seek you today,

I am repenting of lust of the eyes and the pride of life. I confess of the sin of using women in the past and ask you Lord to help me, cover my shame in the name of Jesus. I ask you to forgive me, cleanse me and restore me to the joy of your salvation in Jesus name.

In the name of Jesus, bless me with a good wife who knows how to tell me "no". A woman with a heart totally sold out to you; a heart filled with love and willing to wait until we are in a covenant relationship before we seek intimacy.

Your word says a man who finds a wife, finds a good thing. Lord as you brought a wife to Isaac my father; my prayer is that you bring a wife to me my father in Jesus name.

I bind the spirit of witchcraft, sorcery and divination of the strange woman/man in the name of Jesus.

I bind the spirit of bewitchment in the name of Jesus

I bind the spirit of lies, manipulation and deceit in Jesus name

I bind the spirit of Leviathan and marine spirits in the name of Jesus

I bind the spirit of lust and debauchery in Jesus name

I bind the spirit of whoredom and harlotry in Jesus name

I bind the spirit of rejection and fear in the name of Jesus

I bind the spirit of loneliness/sadness in the name of Jesus

I bind the spirit of masturbation and fantasies in Jesus name

I bind the spirit of pornography in the name of Jesus

I bind the spirit of perversion in the name of Jesus

I bind the spirit of cybersex and peep shows in Jesus name

I bind the spirit of impatience in the name of Jesus

I bind the compromising spirit in the name of Jesus

I bind the spirit of one-night stands in Jesus name

I bind the sex addicted and drug addicted spirit in Jesus name

I bind the hanging out with the (people, fellows) spirit with the sole purpose to drink, smoke, use drugs and expose my life to perversion in Jesus name.

Father God in the name of Jesus keep my heart from deceptive enchanters, siren spirits and deceivers sending and projecting into my mind and emotions what is not of you. I bind every spirit Leviathan and marine spirit in the name of Jesus. My father in the name of Jesus protect me from deception, bewitchment and manipulation. Hide me under the shadow of your wings from seducing spirits, spirits of lust and lies in Jesus name.

Teach me my father how to be a man of God. Bring mentors around me to teach me how to be a man. I ask for guidance and instruction on how to be a man of God ready to be a husband. Teach me how to take care of a wife, how to provide for my home and love my wife.

My father teach me the secret of a woman's heart. Teach me what it is to love my wife unconditionally. Teach me how to show compassion, sincerity and tenderness to my wife. Lord, where I am weak my father help me to see.

Give me the sensitivity to know and understand the secrets of her heart in the name of Jesus. Let me love her so much that I can discern her thoughts, how she is feeling at any particular moment in Jesus name. My Lord heighten my sensitivity to my wife that there is nothing standing between us when you bring wife and us together as husband and wife.

Lord, I ask you today by faith for my soul mate, the woman you created just for me in Jesus name. As I wait on you my father, protect my heart until you send the right women you have chosen for me. My father release my heart to love the woman you have chosen for me. Lord, you are the God of the impossible and nothing is too hard for you, hear my humble prayer today as I wait on you in faith in Jesus name. I release my faith today and wait in expectation for what you have prepared for me in the name of Jesus. (Amen)

Psalms 119:34, Psalms 109:22, Psalms 119:10, Genesis 24:4, Psalms 17:1, 2 Thessalonians 3:5, Romans 5:5 Proverbs 8:34, 1 Kings 8:28, Psalms 88:2, Philippians 1:4, Colossians 1:2, Hebrews 4:12, Hebrews 10:22

Deliverance Prayer – Husband's Responsibility

My father as I come before you on behalf of our men my Lord 1 humbly thank you for teaching them to walk in obedience to the Holy Spirit. Let the Holy Spirit manifest himself in the words that go forth in the name of Jesus. You created the marriage covenant between a man and woman as a commitment to each other and a foundation for families in unity in the name of Jesus. My father The basis of godly Christian marriage requires the death of self; looking back at the old man and being replaced by the new man of oneness in a covenant relationship in the name of Jesus. Father God only through marriage can a man becomes a husband. And my father only through marriage can a woman becomes a wife.

My Father according to **Proverbs 18:22 whoso** findeth a wife findeth a good thing, and obtained favor of the LORD. Father you said there is blessings obtained in getting a godly wife in the name of Jesus.

My father according to 1 Corinthians 11:7

- Father God, the wife is the glory of her husband
- According to Gen 2:18 - the wife is a helper to her husband.

- Ephesian 5:22 – wife is submitted to the husband. In the marriage husband and wife is submitted to each other.

- The wife is to support and uphold the husband

- The wife is to encourage and praise her own husband

- The wife is an intercessor to pray for her husband

- The heart of her husband trust her

- Proverb 31: wife and mother (strength, success and power).

- According to Ephesians 5:29 my father, you have given the husband the role to cherish is wife in the name of Jesus. My father his responsibility is to saturate his wife and children with the word of God. My father the husband is the prophet, priest and king in his home in Jesus name.

My father you created the husband as the head of the marriage and as such, you have given him responsibilities. According to 1 Corinthians 11: 3 and Ephesians: 5:25, a husbands role is to love his wife the way Christ loved the church and gave his life; in the name of Jesus, the husbands responsibility is the head of his household according to 1 Corinthians 11:3. To protect and guard his home through prayers and godly living in Jesus name; to make decisions, support the home and provide direction to wife and children. Lord teach our men, our husband's financial stewardship in the management of money in the name of Jesus.

According to <u>Deuteronomy 30:19</u> | you have set before the man in this covenant relationship set before men life and death, blessing and cursing: therefore choose life, that both thou and thy seed may live: Lord bless our men to choose life and to make right decisions to bring forth blessings over their marriages and homes in Jesus name.

My father, you honor covenant and my father according to **Exodus 20:14** |men shall not commit adultery. The enemy bring in temptation and every work of the flesh, according to **Galatians 5:19** now the works of the flesh are manifest, which are *these*; Adultery, fornication, uncleanness, lasciviousness. Adultery is immorality, which is the breaking of a covenant. Psalm 25:14 – God reveals himself to his people through revelation of his word. **Hebrews 13:4**

My father, you honor covenant and my father 1 pray our men honor their marriage covenant, according, Malachi 2:13-you will not hear their prayers if they walk in disobedience before you. Holy God, you will not hear prayers of the unrighteous, you cannot look at sin, so my father, if our men come before you in pain with an unrepentant heart my father, and you will not hear them in the name of Jesus. My father in the name of Jesus, you do not honor covenant breakers. Unfaithfulness is a breaking of covenant. Adultery is a serious sin so God give our men wisdom in choices they make in the name of Jesus.

My father give our men revelation knowledge through the Holy Spirit, help them to make daily decisions, and avoid trap of deception and bondage of the enemy in Jesus name.

My father teach our men from your word that his role is the head and not the tail above and not beneath in the name of Jesus, according to Deuteronomy 28: 1-28.

Lord the devil deceived our men and placed lies of false expectation that cannot be fulfilled in human strength. The enemy set traps of failure, double standards and internal pressures. Father God our men worship self and not you my father. Self has become their idol in Jesus name.

My father, in the name of Jesus, some husbands are confused, living by hunches, and misinformation and guesses believing the lie of the devil. My father through their disobedience and not following or fulfilling their obligations in the home as husbands, some husbands leave their homes unprotected.

Father God, other husbands have mastered the art of deceit and manipulation. Some husbands cloak pain and brokenness as bravado, machismo refusing to come to you with a broken and a contrite spirit.

In the name of Jesus break bondages and shackles that has been put on them and reveal and expose the pain and suffering in Jesus name. My father heal the gaping open wound of emotional and psychological pain with the blood of Jesus and strengthen them in a time of weakness.

My Father some husbands are walking emotional cripples, emotionally wounded from childhood. These husbands my father have taken on responsibilities and accountability for a marriage and family they are emotionally and psychologically incapable of fulfilling. I pray for these husbands to heal the tear of the devil in the name of Jesus. Bring forth divine healing in the name of Jesus so they are able to stand on their feet spiritually and psychologically as husbands in the name of Jesus name.

In the name of Jesus I plead the blood of Jesus against every demonic spirit that entered their life through disobedience, molestations, child abuse and parental neglect in the name of Jesus. I bind the spirit of rejection and fear in the name of Jesus. I bind the spirit of slavery in the name of Jesus. I bind the spirts of lust, perversion and adultery in the name of Jesus. I bind the spirit of laziness and delinquency of responsibilities in Jesus name.

Father God forgive our men of the sins of omissions that led to the sins of commission in Jesus name. In the name of Jesus; I bind the hand of the enemy that entered through generational curses that came into their lives to bear fruits of irresponsibility, irrational thinking, lacking accountability in the name of Jesus. I bind, rebuke and break the spirit of Jezebel that castrated some husbands in marriages relationships in the name of Jesus. I break the curse now in the name of Jesus.

In the name of Jesus:

I bind the spirit of pride

I bind the spirit of rejection

I bind the spirit of jealousy

I bind the spirit of double mindedness

I bind the spirit of disobedience, rebellion and unbelief

I bind the spirit of generational abandonment

I bind the spirit of emotional/physical and psychological abuse

I bind the spirit of manipulation/lies and deceit

I bind the spirit of infirmity behavioral and deviant spirits

I bind the spirit of lack and poverty

I bind the spirit of laziness

I bind the spirit of slumber

I bind the spirit of idolatry

I bind the spirit of generational harlotry

I bind the spirit of Jezebel

I bind the spirit of lack of responsibility and accountability

In the name of Jesus, I command every spirit named to leave the body of_____ now, never to return in Jesus name.

Father God as our men are delivered teach our men strong family principles to protect home and family.

Teach our men to stand and shoulder whatever comes against the marriage in Jesus name. Father God give our men strength, in the name of Jesus "you are strong- in Jesus name.

My father whatever is bound on earth is bound is heaven, and whatever is lose on earth is lose in heaven. 1 bind every spirt standing in opposition to our men and lose the spirit of the overcomers in their marriages in Jesus name.

My father in the name of Jesus, 1 declare and decree our husbands are free today to walk in their role as prophet, priest and king in their homes in Jesus name. Our men have the boldness to fulfill their responsibilities as husbands by the power and blood of Jesus, in Jesus name. (Amen, Amen)

Genesis 3:6, Genesis 29:32, Proverbs 12:4, Proverbs 31:11, Jeremiah 29:6, Romans 7:2, 1 Peter 3:7, Ephesian 6:1-16, I Timothy 6:4-10, Genesis 2:18, Deuteronomy 28:1-14, 1Peter 2:9, 1 Timothy 4:3, 1 Corinthians 9:26, Proverbs 29:18, James 4:7, Proverbs 23:23, Isiah 54:5, Matthew 19:26, 1 Corinthians 7:16, 1 Corinthians 9:24, Luke 4:18, 2 Timothy 1:7, 1 Corinthians 13:8, 2 Corinthians 6:14, Proverbs 12:11, Hebrews 11:6

Deliverance Prayer for Men

Father God in the name of Jesus, I come to you today in faith, I ask you Father God in the name of Jesus to hear my prayers.

As I intercede on behalf of men, my brothers, nephews and cousins, coworkers and men in my church and community, I plead the blood of Jesus over them now.

I take this authority and speak forth your word in faith in Jesus name; no weapon that is formed against them shall prosper in the name of Jesus. Thank you for your warring angels that is dispatched to protect them and battle on their behalf in the name of Jesus. I bind the strong man over their minds, emotions and thoughts right now in the name of Jesus.

I thank you Father God for giving them all power through your word, giving them authority to trample snakes and scorpions and every work of the enemy in the name of Jesus.

Father God, as Jesus walked on the earth and did mighty works, you have been given them authority through the name of Jesus to do greater works in his name.

According Jeremiah 51:20, thou art my battle-axe and weapons of war and with thee will you break in pieces the nations with thee will you destroy kingdoms, and with thee will you break in pieces the horse and the rider. In addition, with thee will you break in pieces the chariot and him that rideth therein. According to Mark 5:13, Jesus commanded the demons to leave the man with the spirit of legion, and the demons left and was driven into pigs where they drowned in the sea. Father God in the name of Jesus, According Psalms 35:8 – let destruction come upon their enemies unaware that come against our men, and let the nets that they have set into the very net let their enemies fall, let double destruction be the lot of their enemies in the name of Jesus.

In the name of Jesus Christ of Nazareth, I command every spirit, every demon to bow to the name of Jesus:

1 bind the Spirit of Witchcraft, Spirit of Sorcery, Spirit of Divination, Spirit of Bewitchment, Spirit of Judas, Spirit Santeria, Spirit of Obeah in Jesus name, Spirit of slavery, spirit of enslavement, spirit of hopelessness and loneliness in the name of Jesus.

In the name of Jesus, 1 bind the Leviathan Spirit, the spirit of Pride, Spirit of Fear, Spirit of Heaviness, Spirit of Slumber, Spirit of Doubt and Uncertainty.

In the name of Jesus, I bind Spirits of Adultery, Spirit of Fornication and Spirit of Bondage.

In the name of Jesus I bind Spirit of Perversion, Spirit of Legion – unclean spirits, Spirit of Lust, Spirit of Jezebel and Ataliah, Ahab, Python Spirit, the Cobra Spirit, Marine Spirit.

In the name of Jesus I bind the Spirit of Bitterness, Spirit of Depression, spirit of Rejection, Spirit of Sadness/Grief, Spirit of Anger, Spirit of Rage, Spirit of Violence and Murder, Spirit of Rejection, Spirit of Bitterness, Spirit of Drug and Sexual additions, Spirit of Arrested, spirit of idolatry, the spirit of suicide, spirit of laziness, spirit of sadness and depression. Spirit of abandonment, spirit of premeditate murder, Spirits of Behavioral Disorders, Spirit of the Psychopath and Sociopath, Spirit of the Manic and Spirit of the Depressant.

In the name of Jesus I bind Spirit of Molestation, Spirit of Rape, Spirit of Homosexuality, Spirit of Transgender Ambiguity, Spirit of Child Abuse, Spirit of Early Sexual Encounter, Spirit of Sexual Deviants, Spirit of Cutting and Mutilation, Spirit of Emotional and Psychological Strangulation, Spirit of Infirmity, spirit of the soul eater Spirit Fear, Spirit Rebellion. I bind the spirit of shame/defilement/and humiliation. I bind the spirit of discouragement in Jesus name.

In the name of Jesus, I bind Spirit of Double Mindedness, spirits of insincerity, jealousy, malice, rejection and envy.

In the name of Jesus, I bind Spirit of Lack and Poverty, the Spirit of Wastage, Spirit of the Vagabond, Spirit of Homelessness, Spirit of the Dungeon, Spirit of the Devourer, Spirit of Idolatry.

In the name of Jesus, I come against Spirits of Sexual Immorality and soul ties formed during sexual intercourse. I come against Spiritual marriages to the strange woman/man in the name of Jesus. I come against the Spirit of defilement in the name of Jesus. I bind every spirit named by fire and the blood of Jesus, in Jesus name.

Every spirit operating and destroying the lives of men, destabilizing their lives; 1 command every spirit operating bringing in disobedience rebellion and unbelief to bow to the name of Jesus right now, in Jesus name. In the name of Jesus, the lives of men will not follow the evil patterns of the past. I reverse every curse to the pit of hell never to return in the name of Jesus.

Let the enemy be turned back that devised the hurt of men in the name of Jesus. Let the deceptive spirit operating in their lives in secret be exposed by fire in the name of Jesus. According to Ephesians 6; 10- 14: "1 take up the whole armor of God and stand. Loins girth with the truth and the breastplate of righteousness the sword of the spirit, which is the word of God." In the name of Jesus, 1 command the two edge sword of the Lord to cut and paralyze the works of the enemy operation right now in Jesus name.

Father God, in the name of Jesus, according to John 5:14 – you commanded the man after he was delivered to sin no more. Father God according to Proverbs 28:9 – you do not hear the prayers of the wicked it is an abomination to you, so Lord in the name of Jesus, forgive men right now in the name of Jesus. Father God, those who sinned willingly or unwillingly. Lord touch their lives and bring forth transformation now in the name of Jesus.

Father God bring forth true repentance in their lives that they turn away from sin and walk towards you Father God. According to 11 Samuel 11:12-17,

David committed sin before you and Lord in spite of committing adultery and murder; Lord you forgave him. However, Lord there was a consequence to the sin even though he was forgiven. Through David's sin, problems and family conflict did not leave his house, nor leave his family. God teach men that they are accountable for their actions and there are consequences to sin.

Lord give men a heart of true repentance to know that you will forgive, heal and restore them Lord and they must walk through the process in obedience to you.

Father God according to Matt 12:31 – you forgive all sins, where sin abound your grace abound towards our men. Father you are the hiding place for men. Psalms 32:7, you delivered the Hebrew boys and place them in great authority, Father God deliver men from every trap, enticement, every prison enslavement that was set for them in Jesus name.

In the name of Jesus, According to Ezekiel 36:25- : You will sprinkle clean water over men and they shall be clean of all their filthiness, and from all their idols will you cleanse them. Lord a new heart you will give them. A new spirit you will put in them. You will give them a heart of flesh. With your spirit within them you will cause them to walk uprightly before you in the name of Jesus: In the name of Jesus, 1 speak life into men to overcome in the name of Jesus

In the name of Jesus 1 cast out every spirit named, and command them to depart from the lives of men right now to the pit of hell in the name of Jesus.

I destroy and blind the eyes of Satan over men through the blood of Jesus, in Jesus name. I destroy mind numbing and mind controlling spirits through the blood of Jesus in Jesus name. In the name of Jesus, pour out your indignation upon their enemies in Jesus name.

Father God, free men from manipulation and satanic traps, reverse bad reputation, reverse spoken words used to destroy them by the blood of Jesus. Father God in the name of Jesus, destroy the Spirit of Haman operating against men. Destroy the spirit of Judas operating against them in the name of Jesus; destroy and expose evil calibrators in the name of Jesus. In the name of Jesus, I command every spirit to depart to the pit of hell never to return in Jesus name.

Through the blood of Jesus, I seal every vacancy in the lives of men and fill them with power to overcome through the Holy Spirit. Father God in the name of Jesus give men resilience, the ability to bounce back and call on you, strength to withstand temptations and plots of the enemy.

In the name of Jesus, sever illegal contracts, reverse satanic thoughts, and reverse words spoken against their purpose in the name of Jesus.

Father God in the name of Jesus, I declare and decree salvation, restoration, deliverance and healing in their lives today. I declare and decree freedom, liberty, joy, happiness, success, healthy strong marriages, great relationships, restored and transformed lives, new jobs, new careers, new businesses, favor, success, and prosperity. Father God fill men with supernatural power through the Holy Spirit to overcome in this life and be a testimony to their generations for 1000 years in the name of Jesus.

Father God in the name of Jesus, whatever they put their hands to do in alignment to your word and their purpose, Father God, pour out your blessings to prosper and increase in Jesus name. I declare and decree this year men will rise above every situation that so easily beset them. Sadness of the past is replaced with blessings, favor and prosperity. All good things are flowing into their lives according to the promises in your word, in the name of Jesus.

Father God, I seal this prayer now over men through the blood of Jesus Christ of Nazareth. Amen and Amen!

Proverbs18:19, 2 Timothy 1:7 Isiah 61:38, Roman 11:8, Malachi 3:8-11, Jeremiah 51:20, Psalms 109, Isiah 54:17, Psalms 140, Deuteronomy 30:7, Deuteronomy 28:1-14

Isiah 27:1, 2 Timothy 1:7, Romans 8:15, James 1:8, Proverbs 16: 18-19, Isiah 61:3

Deliverance Prayer: Sons and Brothers

Father God in the name of Jesus I bring my conscious, subconscious, and unconscious mind, will, emotions and personality into subjection under the blood of Jesus, in Jesus name.

Father God I come before you confessing the sins of sons and bothers in my generations, and prior generations in Jesus name. Sins of disobedience, rebellion, and unbelief in Jesus name.

Father God I come before you repenting of their sins and ask for their forgiveness in the name of Jesus. In the name of Jesus, I release your power to manifest in their lives. I ask you God to change their mindset. In the name of Jesus, heal them of the pain and hurt suffered at the hands of family members, friends, co-workers, business associates, church members, and leadership.

Father God I come before you right now and intercede on their behalf my father give me clean hands, and a pure heart in the name of Jesus.

In the name of Jesus, I take authority over every demonic spirit that comes into their thoughts to think impure thoughts; I take authority of every thought and bring it into the captivity to the obedience of Christ.

I bind every thought that is not of you Father God; thoughts that are operating in their lives in Jesus name. Father God as you have forgiven them let them forgive themselves of past offenses in Jesus name. I bind the spirit of slavery used to keep African Americans, specifically African American men, of African descent in bondage in the name of Jesus.

Father God I bind Satan and every demonic agent of Satan that comes against the words going forth on behalf of our men in the name of Jesus.

The devil walks about seeking whom he may devour, Father God thank you that you have cleansed me, purified me and sanctified me through your word. I stand in victory today in Jesus name.

In the name of Jesus, I break soul ties that sons and brother have had with former sex partners, unholy relationships, and ex-spouses in Jesus name. I bind the Jezebel spirit, the spirit of Ahab, the Python spirit, the demon of sexual perversion, the spirt of homosexuality, the spirit of legion in the name of

Jesus. I bind the spirit of Jezebel and Ahab in the name of Jesus. I bind the spirt of Leviathan. I send the judgment of God against every enemy that is pursing them and refuse to release them to go in Jesus name.

I bind and paralyze and destroy all spoke words over their lives' words spoken in anger, bitterness and sorrow in Jesus name.

I break down every wall of Jericho that stands as a mountain of sorrow in their lives in the name of Jesus. I command every wall of opposition to fall, never to rise again in Jesus name.

I command the walls of debt, poverty, lack, not enough, bankruptcy _____ to be destroyed forever never to rise again in the name of Jesus.

I command the demon of infirmity (_____) and fear to be bound by the blood of Jesus. No enemy will stand before them in the name of Jesus.

I break generational curses in the name of Jesus; Every spirit of their ancestors going back 1000 years: spirits of Slavery, Destruction, Unbelief, Distrust, Anger, Frustration, Murder, Stubbornness, Humiliation, Shame, Barrenness, Family Breakdown, Defeat, Oppression, Failure, Breakdown, Oppression, Marriage Failure, Destruction, Adultery, Fornication, Financial Insufficiency, Robbery, Theft, Deception,

Mental and Physical Sickness, Abuse, Financial Starvation. In the name of Jesus I bind every spirit named and command you to walk in dry places in the name of Jesus.

I bind the spirit of the assignment demon whose sole purpose: isolate and separate, lose personal identity, and self-esteem; I send the fire of God and destroy by fire every work of the enemy in Jesus name.

I bind every seed of destruction, sent against brothers and sons; 1 cancel the assignment right now in the name of Jesus. 1 reverse every curse spoken against them and cast every curse to the ground, burn to ashes in Jesus name.

I bind the spirit of rejection in the bloodline in Jesus name.

I bind the works of witchcraft, sorcery, divination, fortune telling, santaria, obeah ungodly intercessory prayers, unholy covenants, candle burnings, incense, powers of darkness, and spiritual wickedness in Jesus name.

I bind the accident-prone spirit in the name of Jesus.

I bind the spirit of Bewitchment in Jesus name. I bind the spirit of Fear and all its cohorts in Jesus name. In the name of Jesus: I bind the spirit of parental abandonment,

I bind the spirit of helplessness, I bind the spirit of slavery/bondage, I bind the spirt of lies and deception, I bind the spirit of pride, I bind the spirit of fear, I bind the spirit of double-minded, I bind the spirit of heaviness, I bind the spirit of infirmity, I bind the spirit of rejection, I bind the spirit of jealousy, I bind the spirit of bondage, I bind the spirit of homelessness, I bind the spirit of wastage, I bind the spirit of sexual addiction, I bind the spirit of idolatry, I bind the spirit of generational polygamy, I bind the spirit of jealousy/malice/hatred and grudge.

I command every spirit other than the Holy of God operating in their lives to be bound right now in Jesus name.

In the name of Jesus, I send the blood of Jesus into their lives to protect them as they go about their day; protect their minds, protect their families, protect their jobs, protect their careers, their businesses, protect their financial life, protect their health in the name of Jesus.

I send the blood of Jesus against sickness, disease, pestilence and infirmity and command you to dry up from the root in the name of Jesus. I lose the blessings over sons and brothers according to Deuteronomy 28: -14.

I declare and decree life, health and strength in the land of the living in the name of Jesus.

Father God you called Abraham, to go to a land he did not know, and he went in obedience; Father God bless brothers and sons to walk in obedience to receive your blessing in Jesus name.

Father God sons and brother choose to fully surrender to you today and all the days of their lives; Father God you lead and guide them as they walk in this life in Jesus name.

In the name of Jesus, I thank you for complete surrender of their lives to you Lord Jesus; keep them under the blood of Jesus in humility, submission to you.

I seal this prayer in the blood of Jesus, in the name of Jesus. Amen!

I Samuel 15:23, Micah 5:12, Nahum 3:7, Galatians 5:12, Leviticus 19:31, Isiah 8:19, Philemon 1:4, Ephesian 1:16, 1 Timothy 2:1, 2 Timothy 1:3, 1 Peter 3:12, Genesis

6:2, Psalms 4:2, Psalms 16:7, Psalms 33:13, Psalms 106:38, Proverbs 28:19, Ecclesiastes 9:12, Isiah 45:11, Hebrews 12:7, James 2:9, 2 Peter 3:1, 1 John 3:12, Jude 1:16, Jeremiah 9: 2-6, Romans 11:8, Isiah 19:14

Deliverance Prayer against the Spirit of Turmoil and Confusion

My father your promise to keep me in perfect peace, because my mind is stayed on you, because I trust in you." Isaiah 26:3.

I thank you my father you are my peace in the midst of the storm and you promise never to leave me nor forsake me in my time of need.

I praise and honor you Lord Jesus that you are my savior and king; you are the one true God, the deliverer and the wings of safety.

I come against the spirit of destruction, the spirit of confusion and the spirit of fear in the name of Jesus.

In the name of Jesus, I come against the spirit of turmoil and confusion that was sent against my life to derail my progress. The hand of the enemy sent angels of destruction to bring in distress to my life; I paralyze the works of the enemy by the blood of Jesus.

Every confederacy formed against my life the blood of Jesus is against you now.

In the name of Jesus I drive out every manifestation of your power that was sent to bring in destruction into my life your works is destroyed right now by the blood of Jesus.

I bind the spirit of turmoil and frustration in Jesus name

I bind the spirit of anxiety, doubt and overwhelmed in the name of Jesus

I bind the childish and immature spirit in the name of Jesus

I bind the spirit of manipulation and deceit in Jesus name

I bind the emotionally distressed spirit in Jesus name

I bind the spirit of panic in Jesus name

I bind the inactive spirit in Jesus name

I bind chain problems in Jesus name

I bind distraction in the name of Jesus

I bind outside interference in the name of Jesus

I bind the spirit of witchcraft, sorcery and divination

I bind the spirit of Leviathan and the marine spirit in the name of Jesus

I bind the spirit of the dragon in Jesus name

I bind the spirit of lust/perversion and deviant spirits in the name of Jesus

I bind the spirit of destiny killers in the name of Jesus

I bind the spirit of shame/disgrace and humiliation in the name of Jesus.

I bind the spirit of financial destruction in Jesus name

I bind the spirit of infirmity (health problems, body, mind and spirit) in Jesus name.

I bind the spirit of unemployment and underemployment in the name of Jesus

I bind the spirit of unfair pay and benefits in the name of Jesus.

I bind the spirit of family destruction (marriage, children etc.,) in Jesus name

I bind the spirit of injustice and discrimination in Jesus name

I bind the spirit of bigotry and prejudice in Jesus name

I bind the vagabond and homeless spirit in the name of Jesus.

I bind the spirit of the devourer in the name of Jesus

I bind the spirit of idolatry in the name of Jesus

My father let the **peace of God rule in my hearts with all wisdom let the songs and psalms be in my heart at all times, my father I will give** thanks to God the Father through your name Jesus Colossians 3:15-17

Lord you gave me peace" my peace I give to you; not as the world gives do I give to you. **Let not your heart be troubled...."** John 14:27

My Jesus, you told me not to be "Be anxious for nothing, but in everything by prayer and supplication, with thanksgiving, let your requests be made known to God; and **the peace of God, which surpasses all understanding, will guard your hearts and minds through Christ Jesus**." Philippians 4:6-7

My father in the midse of tribulation; you told me to be of good cheer, you have overcome the world." John 16:33

"Be still and know that I am God!" Psalm 46:10

By the blood of Jesus, I cast down the carnal mind, which is an enmity against God; for it is not subject to the law of God, nor indeed can be. So then, those who are in the flesh cannot please God, but you are not in the flesh but in the Spirit, if indeed the Spirit of God d1lls in you. Now if not anyone has the Spirit of Christ, he is not His. And if Christ is in you, the body is dead because of sin, but the Spirit is life because of righteousness. Roman 8: 6 – 10. My father as you raised up Jesus from the dead destroy every spirit that is warring against my life. The Life of Jesus dwell in me, the Spirit of Him who raised Jesus from the dead dwells in me, He who raised Christ from the dead will also give life to my mortal body through His Spirit who dwells in me. "Romans 8:6-11

Isaiah 27:1 "In that day the Lord will punish Leviathan the fleeing serpent, with His fierce and great and mighty sword, even Leviathan the twisted serpent; and He will kill the dragon who lives in the sea." In the name of Jesus, I bind all marine spirits.

I command every spirit named bound in the name of Jesus. I command you in name of Jesus to leave the body of this man/this woman and never return in Jesus name. In the name of Jesus, I reverse every curse, every demonic power, and every principality back to the pit of hell now in Jesus name.

This day my father, I will dwell in the secret place of the most high and hide under the shadow of the Almighty today and always in Jesus name. (Psalms 91) (Amen, Amen)

Deliverance Prayer against Deception and Manipulation

My father in the name of Jesus, I come against the spirit of deception and the spirit of manipulation operating in my life in Jesus name. I bind <u>aggressive</u> intentions and behaviors.

I bind the spirit of mammon and the spirit of greed in Jesus name. I bind the spirit of pride in the name of Jesus.

Father your word says "Be not deceived; God is not mocked: for whatsoever a man soweth, that shall he also reap (Galatians 6:7). Therefore my Lord, deliver me from the spirit of deception in the name of Jesus.

Lying lips [are] abomination to the LORD: but they that deal truly [are] his delight. (Proverbs 12:22)

In the name of Jesus, keep me from speaking falsely against my friends and those closely associated with me. "Be not a witness against thy neighbor without cause; and deceive [not] with thy lips." (Proverbs 24:28

Father God in the name of Jesus I plead the blood of Jesus against the manipulating spirit, "Even so ye also outwardly appear righteous unto men, but within ye are full of hypocrisy and iniquity." (Matthew 23:28)

I bind the demon Leviathan and all marine spirits in the name of Jesus. "Thou breakest the heads of leviathan in pieces, *and* gavest him *to be* meat to the people inhabiting the wilderness." (Psalms 74:14)

I bind the spirit of the charmer and enchanter in the name of Jesus. (Deuteronomy 18: 10-11)

I bind the cyber-sex spirit in the name of Jesus

I plead the blood of Jesus against the spirits of superficial charm, emotional blackmail, guilt and threats.

I bind the spirit of lust and seduction in Jesus name.

I bind the spirit of praise and flattery in Jesus name.

I bind the deceiving spirit in the name of Jesus.

I bind the spirit of fear and the climate of fear in the name of Jesus.

I bind the spirit of Jezebel and Ahab, I bind demonic prophetic sayings, I bind witches and wizards, workers and demonic agents of the devil in the name of Jesus, by the blood of Jesus, and I bind the spirit of unholy soul ties and contrary spirits in Jesus name.

I bind the lying spirit, lies of omission in Jesus name.

I bind the cheating spirit in Jesus name.

I bind the deceiving spirit not allowing me to see the lies.

I bind the spirit of denial.

I bind the spirit of evasion in Jesus name

I bind the spirit of shame/guilt and self-pity in Jesus name.

I bind the spirit of a victim playing the victim in the name of Jesus.

I bind and cancel spoken words used to mask the true intent in the name of Jesus.

I BIND THE SPIRIT OF REJECTION IN JESUS NAME

I bind the spirit of parental abandonment in Jesus name

I bind the spirit of generational abandonment in the bloodline in Jesus name

I bind the spirit of neglect in Jesus name

I bind the demonic spirit of projection used to blame others in the in Jesus name.

I bind the spirit of pretense using the victim as a ploy to question his or her judgment in Jesus name.

I bind the spirit of confusion playing dumb to confuse the victim in Jesus name.

I bind the spirit of anger and the spirit of rage in Jesus.

I bind the spirits of deception, beguilement, deceit, bluff, mystification and subterfuge and lies in the name of Jesus.

I bind the spirits of betrayal and violation in the name of Jesus.

In the name of Jesus, I paralyze words spoken against me, I paralyze and destroy vain imagination and thoughts that are not the words of God in the name of Jesus.

I bind and destroy the works of evil sent against me, witchcraft, sanitaria, obeah, evil covenants, divination and sorcery, candle burning and jinxes in the name of Jesus. I plead the blood of Jesus over my life, my spirit soul and body in the name of Jesus.

I declare and decree no dark powers of evil have any control of me; I am covered by the blood of Jesus in the name of Jesus.

My father, I thank you this day, I am free from the spirit of manipulation, manipulators, and deception in the name of Jesus. Who the son has set free is free indeed, by the blood of Jesus and the name of Jesus. (Amen)

Galatians 5:19 - 21, Matthew 7:15, John 8:44, Job 13:7, Jeremiah 26:3, Job 27:4, Psalms 5:6, Psalms 24:4, Psalms

38:12, Psalms 140:11, Psalms 52:2, Proverbs 12:5, Psalms 109:2, 2Timonty 3: 1-5, Ephesian 6:10-18, Matthew 10:28, I Timothy 4:1, Ecclesiastes 8:11, Isiah 1:16, Proverbs 17:13, Jeremiah 9: 2-6

Prayers against Adultery/Infidelity/Sexual Sins

Father God in the name of Jesus, I repent of the sins of disobedience, and rebellion I the name of Jesus. I repent of sexual sins committed against my body and against you father in the name of Jesus.

> I ask you to hear my prayer today Lord, you do not hear the prayers of sinners so God 1 ask for forgiveness, cleanse me of every secret sin in the name of Jesus. Father God I face health risks, financial problems, shattered relationships or even arrest because of risky behaviors and sexual sins against my body. "Thou shalt not commit adultery." (Exodus 20:14)

"And the man that committed adultery with [another] man's wife, [even he] that committed adultery with his neighbour's wife, the adulterer and the adulteress shall surely be put to death." (Leviticus 20:10). Flee fornication. Every sin that a man doeth is without the body; but he that committed fornication sinneth against his own body".(I Corinthians 6:18) "Now the works of the flesh are manifest, which are [these]; Adultery, fornication, uncleanness, lasciviousness, (Galatians 5:19)

Father God by my disobedience the doors of evil has been open against us giving demons access to my home and relationship. Father God in the name of Jesus, I renounce witchcraft, sorcery, divination and any occult exposure I have allowed to enter our lives through disobedience and rebellion and unbelief.

My father through the blood of Jesus, I paralyze the works of the devil right now in Jesus name. I bind agents of Satan, 1 bind the spirits of Jezebel the spirit of Ahab, the spirit of Ataliah. I bind Leviathan and marine spirits in the name of Jesus. I bind the spirit of lust. I bind the spirit of orgies and sex parties in Jesus name. I bind the spirit of astral sex in Jesus name. I bind the cybersex demon in Jesus name.

I bind the spirit of adultery and sexual perversion. I bind the spirit of slavery and enslavement in the name of Jesus. I bind the sex addicted and drug addicted spirits in the name of Jesus. I bind the spirit of pornography. I bind the spirit of prostitution in the name of Jesus. I bind the python spirit in the name of Jesus. I bind the enchanter and siren spirit in the name of Jesus. I bind the comprising spirit in the name of Jesus. I bind the seducing spirit in the name of Jesus. I bind the spirit of death and destruction in the name of Jesus. 1 bind and cancel curses sent against me by demons and principalities in the name of Jesus.

I bind the spirit of rebellion and unbelief in the name of Jesus

I bind the spirit of fear in the name of Jesus

I bind the spirit of idolatry in the name of Jesus

I bind the spirit of jealousy in the name of Jesus

I bind the spirit of polygamy in the bloodline in the name of Jesus

I bind the perverse spirit in Jesus name

I bind the seducing spirit in the name of Jesus

I bind the spirit of slumber in the name of Jesus

I bind the spirit of parental neglect in the name of Jesus

I bind the spirit of abandonment in

Holy Ghost power burn out sin the carnal nature/ inordinate nature that easily bombard my mind in the name of Jesus. 1 plead the blood of Jesus against temptation/sexual fantasies in the name of Jesus.

I plead the blood of Jesus against the strong man operating in my minds and hearts blocking the word of God in the name of Jesus.

I bind the strongman of sexual addictions by the blood of Jesus, in Jesus name.

I bind each spirit named and command you to come out with all your roots, now, in the name of Jesus. In the name of Jesus, by the power in the name of Jesus Christ, go, to the pit of hell in the name of Jesus name.

I plead the blood of Jesus against sexual enticement of the strange woman/man in the name of Jesus. In the name of Jesus I come against every spirt of marriage destruction in the name of Jesus. I command you to be paralyzed, dry up to the root in the name of Jesus.

Father God in the name of Jesus pour divine acid on the seducing spirits sent to lure spouses from each other in Jesus name. In the name of Jesus, by the blood of Jesus seal every door opened by careless words or actions by the blood of Jesus.

In the name of Jesus, our spouses are sealed with the blood of Jesus therefore, demonic polrs cannot penetrate the blood line in the name of Jesus.

Demonic creams and lotions used as love potions to lure and seduce; I cancel and paralyze your powers by the blood of Jesus in Jesus name.

In the name of Jesus, I command total destruction to the Jezebel and Ahab spirit in the name of Jesus.

In the name of Jesus, 1 cancel the anti -marriage spirit in Jesus name. Father God in the name of Jesus let the resurrection power fall to ignite godly marriages in the body of Christ in Jesus name. Let the grave clothes fall off marriages in the name of Jesus. Father God raise the dry bone of marriages and bring in new life in Jesus name. (Ezekiel 37:1-14)

Father God I declare rebellion in the 2nd heaven and send the fire of God against spirits of marriage destruction in the name of Jesus.

In the name of Jesus as Agag was hacked to pieces by Samuel, angels with swords of fire go into the 2nd heaven and hack to pieces every spirit destroying marriages and families in Jesus name.

In the name of Jesus as David cut off the head of Goliath, cut off the head of every strange woman/ strange man mitigating against our marriages in the name of Jesus.

Let the spirit of marriage interference be stopped by fire, in the name of Jesus. Burn to ashes the words spoken and sent as a curse against Christian marriages in the name of Jesus.

In the name of Jesus as Jehu commanded the eunuchs to throw Jezebel down and her blood spilled on the wall and was trodden under foot, so shall it be for every Jezebel coming again my life, my family, my dreams and vision in the name of Jesus. (11 Kings 9:32-33). By the blood of Jesus, the carcass of the Jezebel spirit will be dung in the name of Jesus (11Kings 9:37). Let the zeal of Jehu bring destruction to Jezebel and Ahab spirits, witchcraft and divination in the name of Jesus (11Kings 9:1-10). In the name of Jesus as the house of Ahab was cut off in one day sever the oppressing spirits and agents of demons in Jesus name.

In the name of Jesus, every enemy of marital success, happiness, joy, and peace be destroyed now by the sword of the Lord in the name of Jesus.

Father God I thank you for complete restoration of my marriage. My father what you have joined let no enemy put asunder in the name of Jesus. Amen, Amen.

11 Corinthians 6:4, Luke 10:19, Hebrews 10:35, Matt 10:26, Psalms 37:1, Mark 11:24, Jeremiah 33:3, Isiah 54:17, Hebrews 12:, Joel 2- 25-26, Songs of Solomon 1:2, Songs of Solomon 3: - 1-2, Songs of Solomon 8: 6-7, Samuel 3: 42- 43, Lamentation 5:5, Romans 8:1-2, Romans 8:6-13, I Timothy 6:6-19, 1 Timothy 2: 22-26 Isiah 27:1

Prayers against Marital Strongholds/Oppression

Father God in the name of Jesus, I praise and lift you up right now and honor you for being God.

I bring my mind, body will and emotions under the subjection of the Holy Spirit in Jesus name.

Father God manifest your power through the words I speak, my confession in Jesus name. Let the words of my mouth be acceptable in thy sight today, as I enter into deliverance prayer in the name of Jesus.

Holy spirt fire burn up the works of the devil and his scheme of trickery and deception in my life in the name of Jesus.

Let the fire of God roast to ashes the spirit of hiding and deception and compromise of the enemy in the name of Jesus.

Let the fire of God destroy paralyze the spirit of lies the lying spirit. I command the spirit to die now in the name of Jesus, never to rise again. I bind leviathan and all marine spirits in Jesus name.

I bind the demon of lust and the demon of perversion in the name of Jesus.

I bind the demon leviathan and marine spirits in the name of Jesus.

I bind the spirt of harlotry and prostitution in Jesus name.

I bind the spirit of epilepsy in the name of Jesus

I bind the spirit of molestation and sexual abuse in the name of Jesus.

I bind generational curses and spoken words over my marriage in the name of Jesus.

I bind the spirit of incest and sibling sexual exploration in Jesus name.

I bind the spirit of witchcraft sorcery and divination in the name of Jesus.

I bind the spirit of bewitchment in the name of Jesus

I bind the spirit of demonic sexual fantasies in the name of Jesus

I bind the spiritual husband and spiritual wife in the name of Jesus. I bind the spirt of masturbation in the name of Jesus.

I bind the spirit of slumber in the name of Jesus

I bind the spirit of jealousy in the name of Jesus

I bind the spirit of bondage in the name of Jesus

I bind the spirit of fear in the name of Jesus

I bind the spirit of unbelief in the name of Jesus

I bind the spirit of envy in the name of Jesus

I bind the spirit of grudge in the name of Jesus

I bind the spirit of parental neglect in the name of Jesus

I bind the spirit of necromancy in the name of Jesus

Father God sanctify my eyes and heart to meditate on the word of God in the name of Jesus. I bind the demons of homosexuality, lesbianism and pornography in the name of Jesus. Father God every spirit giving life to homosexuality or pornography burn to ashes in the name of Jesus. Father God every sexual act giving demons access to a spirit of homosexuality be paralyzed, die now in the name of Jesus.

Father God in the name of Jesus sanctify and cleanse the marriage bed by your blood in the name of Jesus. Father God what you have joined together my father let no man, no woman, no demon put asunder in the name of Jesus. Amen and Amen

2 Corinthians 10:4, Isiah 54:17

Psalms 119:134, Psalms 116:3, Psalms 42:9, Isiah 30:12

Romans 12:20, Matthew 10:28, 1 Peter 2: 1- 25, Isiah 28:18, Galatians 5:20, Isiah 8:19, Deuteronomy 4:18

Romans 8:26, 2 Corinthians 6:14, Romans 10:17, Hebrews 4:12, Ezekiel 18:4, Ezekiel 12:24, 2 Thessalonian 2:9, Deuteronomy 18:11

Prayers against Marital Destruction

Father God in the name of Jesus, 1 pray peace, joy and happiness for my marriage that was designed and fashioned by you in the name of Jesus. My father I pray that you intercede in my marriage right now; change the atmosphere in my home and marriage in Jesus name.

You are God my father and nothing is too hard for you. Father God 1 cast not away your confidence in my marriage as it has a great recompense of reward in Jesus name. (Hebrews 10:35).

In the name of Jesus, I bind the spirit of witchcraft, sorcery and divination sent against the marriage as a weapon of destruction. I bind the spirit of Jezebel the harlot in Jesus name.

I send the fire of God and plead the blood of Jesus against the strange man or strange woman opposing the marriage in the name of Jesus (Proverbs 2:6). In the name of Jesus, I send the plagues of leprosy against the enemies mitigating against my spouse and I. Enemies sent against my marriage and family in the name of Jesus (Leviticus 13:2-3).

In the name of Jesus every dragon that comes against my marriage is destroyed by the blood of Jesus. "And Hazor shall be a dwelling for dragons, [and] a desolation forever: there shall no man abide there, nor [any] son of man dwell in it". Jeremiah 49:3. Father God in the name of Jesus, every viper and snake sent to poison the marriage; I reverse the poison back to sender 100 folds. Let the judgment of God according to Psalms 140 destroy health, family and finances of demonic agents of Satan in Jesus name.

As worms eat up dead things, let the leprosy eat their flesh so there is no rest to the wicked in the name of Jesus (Leviticus 13:44-57). "And immediately the angel of the Lord smote him, because he gave not God the glory: and he was eaten of worms, and gave up the ghost". (Act 12:23)

By the blood of Jesus, let the plague that fell upon the children of Egypt fall upon marital enemies in Jesus name (Exod. 12:28-30).

"And it came to pass that night that the angel of the LORD went out, and smote in the camp of the Assyrians an hundred fourscore and five thousand: and when they arose early in the morning, behold, they [were] all dead corpses." 11Kings 19:35

I plead the blood against my marital enemies so that their flesh loose running issue without day and night in the name of Jesus (Lev15:3-4).

In the name of Jesus, I send the judgment of God according to Psalms 140 against words spoken in opposition to martial success, words spoke as a cure, by enemies and satanic agents reverse them back to sender in the name of Jesus.

In the name of Jesus, I come against idle vows, and demonic confederacy made against my marriage.

Father God send the judgment of King Asa on all enemies who oppose and stand as a giant in my life in the name of Jesus.

In the name of Jesus, I command total destruction in the camp of my marital enemies today in the name of Jesus.

In the name of Jesus, I bind the spirits of witchcraft, divination and sorcery in Jesus name. I bind the spirits of malice, jealousy, malice envy and hatred in the name of Jesus.

I bind the perverse spirit

I bind the seducing spirit

I bind the spirit of slumber

I bind the spirit of pride

I bind the spirit of bondage

I bind the spirit of enslavement

I bind the spirit of rejection/shame

I bind the spirit of discouragement

I bind the spirt of lies and deception

I bind the spirit of fear

I bind the spirit of Jezebel

I bind the spirit of Lust

I bind the spirit of rebellion

I bind the spirit of unbelief

I bind the spirit of abandonment

I bind the spirit of frustration and bitterness

I bind familiar spirits

In the name of Jesus, let the blood of Jesus slam shut every entrance and exit of marital interference from families and demonic friends sending words as curses into the marriage in Jesus name.

In the name of Jesus, 1 declare and decree joy, peace and happiness, flow as a river of marital bliss in the name of Jesus.

Thank you God for marital restoration, thank you Lord for love, peace and joy in the marriage in Jesus name.

My father you do not make mistakes so my father help me to stand and do what I need to so to fix the mess I made by making foolish choices and alignment with the wrong people in Jesus name. Lord I ask you to help me to do what you have asked me to do. Help me my father to walk in obedience before you in the name of Jesus.

My Lord help me to stand as the man of God you have called me to be, help me to speak the truth in love. Help me today my father never to look back, and look to you as my source of strength in my weakness in the name of Jesus.

Today, I declare my marriage and relationship is blessed, favored and empowered to succeed and grow in Jesus name. I declare new life according Joel 2:25-26 total restoration. My father what you have joined let no man, no woman no demon put asunder in Jesus name. (Amen and Amen).

Leviticus 19:31, Isiah 8:19, Exodus 22: 18, Ephesian 6: 10:14, I Peter 3:7, Proverbs 18:22, Proverbs 10:12, Galatians 5: 19- 21, 1 Corinthians 6:9, John 8:44

2 Corinthians 6:14, 18, Genesis 2:24, 2 Chronicles 7:14. Malachi 2:16, I Corinthians 7: 10- 11. Matthew 5: 31-32, Genesis 2:24, Isiah 27:1, Jeremiah 9: 2-6, Romans 11:8

Intense Warfare prayers: Prayers for Behavioral disorders: this may be interesting for some however, it is important to understand behavioral disorders and emotional disorders from a layman's term.

Schizophrenia, ADHD, Psychopaths, Narcissist

Narcissists: (Male and Female)

Manipulation, covert manipulation, idealization, devaluation, Abandonment

Who are they: Narcissist think they are perfect everyone else is beneath them? The identity of a narcissist is an illusion. Superficial, the classic case of a Jekyll and Hyde personality. They idealize and deep dive into relationships prematurely. Lack boundaries in relationship and friendships. "Emotional poverty" - they feel nothing. Lack empathy or compassion. Narcissist destroy whom they cannot control. Methods: degrade, humiliate and damage. Narcissist have a deep-seated hatred of women in case of a man and for a woman a deep-seated hatred of men. They treat their subject as objects; there is no love because they feel nothing. They mimic emotions and copy feeling by observing others. ((Note: The narcissist – idealize a target with attention beyond normal behavior, in other words the subject is put on a pedestal, knocked off then discarded coldly and callously).

(As a group, they are dangerous and should be avoided. Disconnect from any form of interaction whether face to face or on social media. (Lose and run fast)!

Psychopaths/Sociopaths: (Male and Female*)-*

"Anti-social personality disorder

□ regularly breaks or flaunts the law

□ constantly lies and deceives others

□ is impulsive and doesn't plan ahead

□ can be prone to fighting and aggressiveness

□ has little regard for the safety of others

□ Irresponsible, can't meet financial obligations

□ doesn't feel remorse or guilt"

"Psychopathy might be related to physiological brain differences. Research has shown psychopaths have underdeveloped components of the brain commonly thought to be responsible for emotion regulation and impulse control. Psychopaths, in general, have a hard time forming real emotional attachments with others. Instead, they form artificial, shallow relationships designed to be manipulated in a way that most benefits the psychopath. People are seen as pawns to be used to forward the psychopath's goals. Psychopaths rarely feel guilt regarding any of their behaviors, no matter how much they hurt others."

"The sociopathy is the result of environmental factors, such as a child or teen's upbringing in a very negative household that resulted in physical abuse, emotional abuse, or childhood trauma. Even have families and seemingly loving relationships with a partner. While they tend to be well-educated, they may also have learned a great deal on their own."

"Sociopaths, in general, tend to be more impulsive and erratic in their behavior than their psychopath counterparts. While also having difficulties in forming attachments to others, some sociopaths may be able to form an attachment to a like-minded group or person. Unlike psychopaths, most sociopaths don't hold down long-term jobs or present much of a normal family life to the outside world." World of Psychology "Difference between Psychopaths and Sociopaths" John M. Grohol, Psy.D.

Now that we have a definition of the behavior, types let us deep dive a bit further. What do you do? How do you proceed? Do you run and hide or do you fight in the spirit realm? As the person either married to one of these persons or in a relationship, primarily seek

God for direction before proceeding in deliverance. The faint of heart will pack up and go, and going must be done in a way where the personality is not threatened in any way. Do not confront them! In other words, remain sane, stable, and safe and saved!

Prayer instruction before behavioral and emotional disorder prayer points:

- The fight is not against the person but the spirit operating through them and guiding them in the behavior patterns.
- Every demon spirit must be bound first, you cannot go into a strongman's house without binding the strongman. Therefore locate the strongman first. Next, start progressive prayers. You will begin to see signs that the prayers is bringing forth changes. (If it is at all possible, prayer separate from this person. Do not remain under the same roof or if you are praying seek the support of others to join you in prayers as reinforcement).
- Deliverance prayer against a spirit of legion is progressive, multiple prayers and counseling is needed after the demons have left this person. Do not think this is done and it is over. (Continue

prayers and more so, start counseling to seek outside help to maintain control for a lifetime).

- The new lifestyle must be maintained if not the state of this subject is worse that it was prior. Also as a precautionary note: The chameleon personality will try to fool you.

- The personality is manipulative and vindictive. This personality values reputation and will do all to maintain this good image they created and will not stand back quietly while you try to shatter their world and reputation.

- The personality type is dangerous and this can affect your life, be very careful. Contact the police, your church, get an order of protection. Do what and anything that is necessary to protect your life, your reputation and your finances.

- The angel of the Lord is encamped around you. No weapon that is formed can prosper as a child of God. Be wise as a serpent and harmless as a dove. Do not take unnecessary chances or foolish careless thinking because you are saved. Be obedience listen to the Holy Spirit, seek counsel. Follow the leading of the Holy Spirit and trust him to lead and guide you into all truths. Amen

Prayer against: Arrested Development Syndrome (Dyslexia and ADHD)

Father God in the name of Jesus, let the word from my mouth be acceptable in thy sight today as I come before you in humility and submission. Wash my heart, my mind, my will and emotions with your blood. I declare and decree total protection over my family and possessions by the blood of Jesus. My father, cover me in the blood of Jesus from the top of my head to the tip of my toes as I enter into deliverance prayer.

In the name of Jesus, I declare war in the camp of the enemy of arrested development syndrome in Jesus name. I come against the spirits of psychological manipulation, the spirit of physical manipulation, Dyslexia, ADHD in Jesus name. I bind these spirits by the blood of Jesus. I bind the strongman of arrested development syndrome. I bind the strongman and cohort responsible for the psychological and physical manifestation in the name of Jesus. In the name of Jesus, I bind spirits of witchcraft, sorcery, and divination in Jesus name. I bind the spirit of infirmity in the name of Jesus. I bind the spirit of rejection and fear in the name of Jesus. I bind the spirit of Leviathan and marine spirits in the name of Jesus. I bind spirits of lust, perversion and legion – unclean spirits in the name of Jesus. I bind the parasitic spirit in the name of Jesus. I bind the python and cobra spirit in the name of Jesus. I bind the sexually addicted and drug addicted spirits in Jesus name.

I bind the spirit of hearing voices and familiar spirits in the name of Jesus. I bind the selfish and self- centered spirit in the name of Jesus. I bind the repetitive spirit in the name of Jesus. I bind the childish, immature spirit in the name of Jesus. I bind the out of control spirit in the name of Jesus. I bind the manipulative, lying and deceitful spirits and their co-horts in the name of Jesus. I bind the spirits of competition and attention seeking in Jesus name.

I command each and every spirit name by the blood Jesus to leave _____now. I command every demon hiding and giving rise to the spirit of legion to come out now in the name of Jesus.

In the name of Jesus, I command every entry and exit point closed by the blood of Jesus. In the name of Jesus, I command divine reversal to the womb of the point of entry _____. I bind the spirits to die now in Jesus name.

Father God in the name of Jesus, fill every vacancy in the life of_____ with your power by the Holy Spirit in Jesus name. Let the blood of Jesus destroy and annihilate years of childish behaviors, childish speech and childish thought pattern and childish behaviors in the name of Jesus.

In the name of Jesus, I release the blood of Jesus to restore the years that the locust and cankerworm has eaten in my life in the name of Jesus. In Jesus name, restore age _____adult normal emotional behaviors, adult age __ speech, adult__ age related thought pattern including emotional accountability and a responsibility in Jesus name.

Father God restore the lost years to_____from __ to ___ in Jesus name. By the blood of Jesus accelerate the growth process so ___ is able to reason at _____ age level in Jesus name.

Father God _____ is able to process information at age _ in Jesus name.

In the name of Jesus, I command a new mind, a new heart, a new thinking pattern according to your word in the name of Jesus.

Lord thank you for a miracle today _____ is able to reason, speak and is accountable at __ age level in the name of Jesus.

My father nothing is too hard for you and 1 rest in your care today. 1 will call forth a miracle today and believe you for what 1 do not see with my natural eyes, however through the eyes of faith 1 embrace the transformation.

1 declare_____ a new life today restored by the po1r and blood of Jesus Christ of Nazareth o Jesus name, Amen.

John 5:5, Hebrews 5:2 Luke 13:12, Roman 6:19, Romans 14:1-23, 22 Chronicles 33:6

Prayer against Behavioral Disorders: Bipolar and Manic Depressant

My father in the name of Jesus, I cover and plead the blood of Jesus over my life, my family and my possessions. I come before you today and bring my body mind, spirit and soul before you as the great physician. In the name of Jesus I bind the spirit of infirmity, heal me today of all diseases and emotional and psychological disorders in the name of Jesus. My father drive away every condition that has come against my mind, personality and my being in the name of Jesus.

In the name of Jesus, I bind, paralyze and cancel every spirit operating and manifesting as bi-polar and manic depressant disorder. I bind the co-hort spirits in Jesus name:

I bind the spirit of fear and confusion.

I bind the spirit of rebellion and rejection.

I bind the spirit of talkativeness.

I bind the spirt of arguing and disagreements.

I bind the spirit of lying.

I bind the spirt of demonic revelations.

I bind the spirit of overly sexual behavior.

I bind the spirit of perversion.

I bind the spirt of promiscuity.

I bind the spirt of fornication and the spirit of adultery.

I bind the spirit of destruction.

I bind the spirit of death

I bind the spirit of leviathan

I bind the spirt of anger.

I bind the spirit of fear.

I bind the spirit of slumber.

I bind the spirit of hopelessness and helplessness.

I bind the spirit of Jezebel and Ahab.

I bind the spirit of lust.

I bind the spirit of witchcraft and divination.

I bind the spirit of sorcery.

I bind the spirit of demonic sayings.

I bind the spirit of hearing voices.

I bind the spirt of lies and deception.

I bind the serpentine and the python spirit.

I call you out by the blood of Jesus. I command you to exit the body of_____(name) now. I command you to walk in dry places until your day of destruction in the name of Jesus.

In the name of Jesus, every vacancy that is now open, I command the blood of Jesus to fill in Jesus name. Holy Spirit fire burn every residue in the life of this person by the fire of the living God in Jesus name. My father create in _____ (name) a clean heart, mind, and spirit in the name of Jesus.

In the name of Jesus, I declare a new life for _____. I declare new speech pattern and new way of thinking.

In the name of Jesus, I declare a new thought pattern. I declare and decree a new life for _____.

In the name of Jesus create and resurrect dead and destroyed brain patterns. Create new normal brain pattern by the blood of Jesus.

In the name of Jesus, restore, resurrect the life of _____ so (he/she) can life a transformed life thinking your thoughts and speaking your words in the name of Jesus.

Let the blood of Jesus Christ, fill every area in _____penetrate and restore from the inside out from this day forth in the name of Jesus. _____ You are a new creation in Jesus name.

Father God let the word of my mouth and the meditation of my heart be acceptable unto you this day. My father let the testimony of your healing manifestation be self-evident for all to see in Jesus name.

I seal this prayer by the blood of Jesus, and declare this is a transformation and blessing that cannot be reversed, in Jesus name. Amen and Amen.

John 5:5, Hebrews 5:2 Luke 13:12, Roman 6:19, Romans 14:1-23, 22 Chronicles 33:6, Ezekiel 12:24

Prayer against Behavioral Disorders, Narcissists, (Sociopath/Psychopath Behaviors)

Father God, in the name of Jesus, I cover my life in the blood of Jesus; I plead the blood of Jesus over my life, possessions and families. My father cover everything that concerns me under the blood of Jesus, in the name of Jesus. My father, "no weapon that is formed against me can prosper in Jesus name" (Isiah 54:17)

In the name of Jesus, I bind the demon strongman spirits of behavioral disorder narcissists, sociopaths and psychopaths. I plead the blood of Jesus against every cohort spirit of behavioral disorder that manifest in my life in the name of Jesus.

My father I pray and ask for forgiveness' in the name of Jesus, I repent of the spirit of forgiveness and rebellion and unbelief.

In the name of Jesus:

I bind the spirit narcissist

I bind the spirit of psychopaths

I bind the spirit of sociopaths

I bind the spirits of Jezebel, Ahab and Atheliah

I bind the spirit of a whore and debauchery

I bind the python spirit

I bind the spirit basilisk

I bind the spirit of witchcraft, sorcery and divination

I bind the occult spirit

I bind false religions in the name of Jesus

I bind the spirit of heresy

I bind the spirit of slavery and enslavement

I bind the spirit of enticement

I bind the spirit of harassment

I bind the spirit of torment

I bind the accusing spirit

I bind the compulsive spirit

I bind the addictive spirit

I bind the spirit of guilt

I bind the spirit of rejection

I bind the spirit of infirmity

I bind the demon spirit Leviathan and marine spirits

I bind the spirit of Legion and unclean spirits

I bind the spirit of perversion

I bind the spirit of slumber

I bind the spirit of early childhood sexual exploration

I bind the spirit of child abuse

I bind the parasite spirit

I bind the spirit of idolatry

I bind the spirit of isolation/ loneliness and self-pity

I bind the spirit of childhood neglect

I bind the familiar spirit

I bind the aggressive spirit,

I bind the spirit of anger and violence

I bind the spirit of murder

I bind the spirit of retaliation

I bind the spirit of emotional destruction

I bind the glib and superficial spirit in Jesus name

I bind the egocentric spirit

I bind the spirit of pride

I bind the spirit of compulsive lying

I bind the spirit of depression

I bind the spirit of exaggeration

I bind the spirit of blasphemy

I bind the unclean speech spirit

I bind the spirit of deception and manipulation

I bind the spirit of hiding

I bind the spirit of abandonment

I bind the spirit of tiredness

I bind the spirit of restlessness

I bind the spirit of suicide

I bind the spirit of resentment and grudge

I bind the spirit of confusion

I bind the spirit of insanity

I bind the spirit of death and murder

I bind the spirit of emotional poverty

I bind the spirit of soul eaters

I bind the spirit that entered in utero

I bind the spirit of deadness of the mind, heart, soul and spirit

I bind the spirit of self -indulgence

I bind the demonic spirit of grandiose dreams and visions

I bind the spirit of fantasy

I bind the spirt lack of conscience

I bind the spirit lack of remorse

I bind the spirit lack of guilt

I bind the spirit of mind control

I bind the spirit of manipulation, cunning and deceit

I bind the spirit lack of empathy

I bind the spirit that debase people

I bind the spirit the treat and see people as objects

I bind the spirit of emotional coldness and callousness

I bind the spirit of impulsiveness and compulsiveness

I bind the spirit of unreliability

I bind the spirit poor behavior control

I bind the spirit that crave excitement

I bind the spirt lack of conscience

I bind the spirit that lack responsibility

I bind the spirit of lies and insincerity

I bind the spirit of cold bloodedness

I bind the spirit of lack of nervousness

I bind the spirit that is easily offended

I bind the hotheaded spirit

I bind the ruthless spirit

I bind the willful and aggressive spirit

I bind the spirit lacking shame

I bind the cold distant and self-sufficient spirit

I bind the spirit of filth

I bind the defiling spirit

I bind the spirit with no moral values

I bind the spirit of temper tantrums

I bind the self- centered Spirit

I bind the predatory reptilian stare in the name of Jesus

I bind the selfish spirit

I bind the spirit of cruelty wanting to see people suffer

I bind the spirit lack of impulse control

I bind the spirit lack of moral reasoning

I bind the overlay sexual spirit in Jesus name

I bind the sexually addictive and drug spirit

I bind the addictive spirit

I bind the spirit of adultery

I bind the spirit of masturbation

I bind the spirit of fornication

I bind the spirit of gluttony

I bind the compulsive spirit

I bind the non-conformist spirit

I bind the spirit that have difficulty with discipline and authority

I bind the spirit of lacking patience

I bind the spirit of easily bored

I bind the spirits of *schizophrenia*, rebellion and rejection

I bind the spirit of strong intuition

I bind the spirit of fortunetelling and the psychic.

I bind the spirit of shallow emotion and emotional poverty

I bind the spirit of wastage

In the name of Jesus, crush the head of every serpentine spirit that crawl and hover in the name of Jesus. In the name of Jesus, I bind the spirit of faulty development. By the blood of Jesus, I speak total destruction to the spirits of psychopath and sociopath and all its cohorts in the name of Jesus.

In the name of Jesus, I speak healing of head trauma that caused damage to the brain in the name of Jesus. I speak life and restoration to physical damage from head trauma in the name of Jesus. In the name of Jesus, I speak healing to any part of the body that with impacted in utero.

In the name of Jesus, every spirit, every demon named, I command you to come out now. I command you to leave the body of_____(name) unharmed in Jesus name.

In the name of Jesus, I command every spirit and demon to return to the pit of hell without delay. By the power in the name of Jesus I command every entrance and exit point closed in the life of (_____). In the name of Jesus, there is an off limits sign placed on their life and sealed by the blood of Jesus, in the name of Jesus.

In the name of Jesus, I lose love, compassion, mercy kindness and consideration for people in the heart of _____ from this day forth. I declare a new heart in _____ (name) in the name of Jesus.

I declare a new mind in _____ (name) in the name of Jesus.

In the name of Jesus I lose _____(name) feeling of love and affection, and caring for special people in his my life.

In the name of Jesus, I lose _____(name) show empathy towards those he loves and all people.

In the name of Jesus, I lose_____ (name) want to take care of those he loves, in the name of Jesus

In the name of Jesus, I lose _____ (name) sacrifice his desires for the care of others in the name of Jesus.

Father God, thank you for a new life, new heart, new brain, new mind, a new spirit and new soul_____(name) in Jesus name.

Father God in the name of Jesus, I command a new heart, new mind, new brains to ___ today in the name of Jesus (Ezekiel 37:6)

In the name of Jesus, I lose a heart to love and take care of people in the name of Jesus. From this day forth __ will no longer see people as objects but will see people through the eyes of Jesus Christ and love, care and cherish them with a clean and loving heart in the name of Jesus.

I declare and decree, a new mind, new soul and new spirit in the name of Jesus. I declare and decree, a new heart, new brain pattern, new emotions, love overflowing In Jesus name. "Let this mind be in you which was in Christ Jesus. "(Philippians 2: 5). In the name of Jesus from this day forth, you are a new creation" old things are passed away behold all things are becoming new", by the stripes and the blood of Jesus of Nazareth.(2 Corinthians 5:17), Amen.

From this day forth_____ (name) walks according to the word of God. Thank you Lord for total surrender to your will and your way, in Jesus name. I declare and decree blessing, the favor of the Lord over your life this day in the name of Jesus (Amen, Amen).

John 5:5, Hebrews 5:2 Luke 13:12, Roman 6:19, Romans 14:1-23, 22 Chronicles 33:6, Leviticus 19:31, Galatians 5: 19 - 25, Philipians 4:8, Jeremiah 44:9, Deuteronomy 21:18-21, Proverbs 22:6, 2 Timothy 3:2, Romans 1:30, 1 Timothy 4:2, James 3:16 – 17, 1 Corinthians 13-4-5, Romans 2:8, Leviticus 19:18, Isiah 56:11, 1 Peter 5:8, Mark 16:18, Luke 10:19, Psalms 58:4, Isiah 27:1, 1 Timothy 4:2, Jeremiah 9" 2-9, Isiah 19:14, Romans 11:8 Romans 8:6, Proverbs 25:28, John 2:16

Prayer against Addictive Spirits: Sexual Addictions, Drug Addictions

Father God in the name of Jesus, I praise and honor you today. Thank you for your amazing grace in my time of need. I bring my life before you my father and ask you to transform my mind, my thinking, my outlook and how I see people in the name of Jesus.

My father your word says if I confess my sins, you are faithful and just to forgive my sins, and to cleanse me from all unrighteousness. (1John 1:9)

Lord I have sinned before you and come asking for forgiveness. My father I have no will of my own I have become enslaved by a condition that has taken over my entire life. This addiction has bankrupt my life. I am enslaved by my passions for (Sex, Drugs etc.).

Lord Jesus, I no longer act on my own anymore, this condition affects my mind, my heart, my will, my emotions and my body. My father I ask you to help me today, I am weak the addiction rack my body day and night. God I humbly come before you now seeking you to heal me completely in Jesus name.

My father I confess, I am an addict. I have no control over _____(Sex or, Drugs). I crave (____) (sex, drugs, name the addiction) all the time. I go looking for it every -where, I use people to meet my need. I have sold my soul because of a carnal nature and need you now my father to break the cycle of destruction in my life.

Father God, I have stolen, cheated and lied to those I love. I have manipulated and deceived my (wife, husband) to get what I needed. I am emotionally callous and only concerned about meeting my selfish needs, I have no concern for anyone else but me. I feel no remorse and guilt for what I am doing, I am emotionally bankrupt.

Lord, I hurt and manipulate my (wife/husband); My father I lost my dignity, I lost my self- esteem and my self- respect. My only desire is to get my appetites satisfied.

My father I have ignored my health and the health of my (wife/husband) and used them for my convenience. I have become selfish, self- seeking and self-serving. I am living in the den of the devil; he has enslaved my life through this addition. I am asking you my father have mercy on me and change my life.

In the name of Jesus, I bind the spirit of addictions in the name of Jesus. (I bind the spirit of _____ addictions in Jesus name. I bind every spirit named in the name of Jesus:

I bind the demon spirit Leviathan and marine spirits

I bind the spirit of lust

I bind the Jezebel and Ahab spirit

I bind the python spirit

I bind the spirit Legion

I bind the spirit perversion

I bind the deviant spirit

I bind the spirit of rejection and parental rejection

I bind the spirit of fear

I bind the spirit pride and arrogance

I bind the spirit of early childhood sexual exploration

I bind the spirit of abandonment

I bind the spirit of child abuse

I bind the spirit of molestation

I bind the spirit of rape and sexual abuse

I bind the spirit of death

I bind the spirit of premeditated murder

I bind the parasite spirit

I bind the spirit of idolatry

I bind the spirit incest

I bind the spirit of fornication and adultery

I bind the spirit of deception and lies

I bind the spirit of witchcraft in Jesus name

I bind the spirit of bewitchment in Jesus name.

I bind the spirit of manipulation in Jesus name

I bind the spirit of deceit and lies

I bind the emotionally callout spirit

I bind the spirit fantasy

I bind the spirit cruelty

I bind the wanton spirit

I bind the spirit of turmoil and confusion

I bind the spirit of idolatry in the name

I bind the drug spirit in Jesus name (if applicable)

I bind the sexual demon in Jesus name (if applicable)

In the name of Jesus I break every chain holding me captive in Jesus name.

In the name of Jesus, I declare healing to head trauma and brain injuries in the name of Jesus.

I cast out every addictive spirit (_____) (name the spirits) in the name of Jesus, I command you to leave my body right now in Jesus name.

Father God as the spirits leave, I command the healing power of the blood of Jesus to fill every vacancy. I command every entrance and exit closed by the blood of Jesus, in the name of Jesus.

I declare and decree by the blood of Jesus a new brain, a new heart, a new mind in____.

In the name of Jesus, _____ is new creature and walk in the newness of Life by the resurrection power that is in the blood of Jesus.

My father you said my sins and iniquities will you remember no more according to (Hebrews 10:17

MY FATHER GOD YOUR WORD SAYS, Blessed ARE they whose iniquities are forgiven, and whose sins are covered. (Romans 4:7). I thank your right now for a restored life.

I thank you for a restored mind, I thank you I now have the mind of Christ.

My father restore unto me the joy of your salvation and renew a right spirit within me in the name of Jesus. From this moment on in the name of Jesus, I am new creations all things are passed away behold all things have become new. (2 Corinthians 5:17)

I seal this prayer by the blood of Jesus, and declare I am healed, delivered and set free in Jesus name.

My father I declare and decree a new life, I love my (wife/husband) I love my family, I love my friends and will no longer feed on them in the name of Jesus.

Thank you my father, think you for a new heart, a new mind, a new spirit, and a new soul. You are God and I praise and thank you for a second chance in Jesus name. (Amen and Amen)

1 John 2:2, John 8: 24, Luke 7:48, Hebrews 10:17, James 4:4, Romans 8:7, 13 Psalms 25:18, Isiah 59:2, Romans 4:7, Proverbs 10:12, 1 Timothy 5:22, I Corinthians 6:18, I Corinthians 10:13, Matthew 5:28, Ephesians 5:5, I Corinthians 7:2, Hebrews 13: 4, Colossians 3:5, 2 Tim 2:22 2 Corinthians 6:14, John 14:15, 1 Corinthians 10:8, Proverbs 5: 18-19, Exodus 20:14, I Corinthians 5:11 Galatians 5: 16-22, Proverbs 5:15, Galatians 5:1

I will bring Health and Cure

Father God in the name of Jesus you are the God of the impossible and nothing is too hard for you, you are the God of all flesh, 1 bring my life and family before you right now and put them under your divine protection according to Psalms 91 in the name of Jesus Christ of Nazareth.

Father God you are the great physician and Lord you will bring health and cure in the barren places in the name of Jesus (Jeremiah. 33:6)

Restore and give life to the dry bones of my life and family cause breath to enter into the dry areas in Jesus name (Ezekiel 37:3-5).

Lord as I speak life to my family and career bring forth flesh upon it in the name of Jesus. (Ezekiel 37:6)

In the name of Jesus, I command my life to come alive, come together, bone to bone in the name of Jesus. (Ezekiel 37:7)

I command the resurrection power of the living God to bring up sinews and flesh upon my life in the name of Jesus (Ezekiel 37:6)

I bind the devil and his cohorts plotting to stop the work in my life and family. In the name of Jesus, I send the judgment of God according Psalms 140 against my unrepentant enemies in the name of Jesus.

In the name of Jesus, I cast down strong delusions and visions from devils. Let the all- consuming fire of the Holy Spirit destroy the camp of evil thoughts and stronghold in process and demonic reasoning in the name of Jesus.

Wind of the Holy Spirit, I command you to come from the 4 corners of the earth and breathe new life up the totality of my being, my family in the name of Jesus.

Holy Spirit power as the 4 winds blow let every door of opportunity that was closed in my life swing open by fire, in the name of Jesus. (Ezekiel 37:10).

By the blood of Jesus, cover the tender plant of my life from the blight of the enemy in the name of Jesus.

In the name of Jesus, open every grave of impossibly in my life and spread out and expand in the name of Jesus. (Ezekiel 37:11-12).

Father God infuse my life with your anointing to do exploits in the name of Jesus. Empower me to grow, to thrive and have dominion over everything I put my hand to do in the name of Jesus.

My Lord in the name of Jesus, let the blessings in your name makes me rich and you add no sorrows to my life or my family (Proverbs 10:22).

My father I believe the thoughts you have for me and my family; thoughts of peace and not evil to give me an expected end, in the name of Jesus (Jeremiah 29:1)

Thank you father God for a restored life in you thank you for rivers of water flowing into my family. In the name of Jesus, I declare and decree the blessings of God over my life and family; my mouth is continually satisfied in Jesus name. Amen, men

Jeremiah 33:6, Jeremiah 32:27, Ezekiel 1-14, Proverbs 3:8, Proverbs 16:24, 3 John 1:2, Psalms 43:5, Isiah 37:17-38.

Prayer against Suicide and Premature Death

Father God in the name of Jesus, I cover my life in the blood of Jesus. I plead the blood of Jesus over my body, mind, will and emotions. I plead the blood of Jesus over my family and possessions in the name of Jesus.

In the name of Jesus, I plead the blood of Jesus against the strongman of destruction in Jesus name. I bind the demon spirit of basilisk (spirit of destruction). I bind the spirit of premature death, suicide and murder in the name of Jesus. "But the children of the murderers he slew not: according unto that which is written in the book of the law of Moses, wherein the LORD commanded, saying, The fathers shall not be put to death for the children, nor the children be put to death for the fathers; but every man shall be put to death for his own sin". (2 Kings 14:6)

I command you strongman basilisk, you spirit of destruction to die now in the name of Jesus. Every spirit that is giving life to an environment to perpetuate premature death I paralyze you now by the blood of Jesus.

You strongman of destruction, I command you to leave _____ in the name of Jesus.

"And as it is appointed unto men once to die, but after this the judgment. (Hebrews 9:27

I bind the spirit of death and suicide in the name of Jesus. "Then Judas, which had betrayed him, when he saw that he was condemned, repented himself, and brought again the thirty pieces of silver to the chief priests and elders Matt 27),

In the name of Jesus:

I bind the spirit of abandonment

I bind the spirit of neglect

I bind the spirit of physical/emotional/psychological abuse

I bind the spirit of mammon, demon spirit over money and the spirit of greed in the name of Jesus. I command every spirit that is not of God to come out with all your roots in the name of Jesus. Blood of Jesus, seal every exit and entry point with the fire of God in Jesus name. "So are the ways of every one that is greedy of gain; which taketh away the life of the owners thereof." (Proverbs 1:19)

I lose life and life more abundantly over myself and family in the name of Jesus.

Father God let the resurrection power of the Holy Spirit destroy and cancel; every spirit pf destruction sent against ___ in the name of Jesus.

In the name of Jesus, I declare you will live and not die and declare the works of the Lord in the land of the living in Jesus name.

Thank you Father God for life. 1 will walk in victory 1 shall live and not die and declare the works of the Lord in the land of the living. In Jesus name (Amen and Amen)

2 Peter 2:1, 2 Thessalian's 5:3, Phil 3:18, 19, Matt 87:17 Jeremiah 17:18, Jeremiah 50:22, Isiah 59:7, Isiah 19:18, Prove 1:27, Proverbs 16:18, Proverbs 10:14, Palm 90:3, Job 5:21, Job 21:1, 1 Corinthians 6:13, Exodus 22:20,

Prayer against Anger (Murder, Violence and Death)

Father God in the name of Jesus, I cover my family and everything that concerns me under the blood of Jesus. I plead the blood of Jesus over my mind, soul and spirit. Father God in Jesus name, I bring men boldly to the throne in Jesus name. I bring African American men before you in Jesus name. Men who are experiencing unfair treatment and injustice in the name of Jesus. Men experiencing strife, impatience, abuse of all kinds, unmet needs, jealousy and every other emotion fueling anger in the name of Jesus. I pull down every stronghold sent against men whatever their color my father, the enemy targeted African American men, to destroy the potential you put in them.

In the name of Jesus, I bind perversion, lust, Jezebel, marine and the spirit of infirmity in the name of Jesus.

In the name of Jesus, I bind the strongman of murder, violence, and death in the name of Jesus. I bind the ruling spirits of suicide, unforgiveness, revenge, cruelty, hate, animosity, jealousy, self-centeredness, greed, hurt, anger bitterness, torture, envy, hostility, long memory, no love, cold love, no mercy, holding grudges, pride and fear in the name of Jesus.

I bind the spirit of anger with fetters from the alter of God and cohorts (hidden anger, rage, poison, rejection, burning with anger, wrath, resentment, bad temper, evil speaking, unrighteousness, slander, contention, heaviness, fury, fire kindles in anger, quarrelling, brawling, clamor, animosity, abusive, blasphemous, language, spite, ill will, malice, and all hidden anger, injustice, fear of confrontation, unmet needs, helplessness, insecurity, control. Vengeance and manipulation in the name of Jesus. In the name of Jesus, I bind the named spirits:

I bind the spirit disobedience and unbelief

I bind the spirit pride

I bind witchcraft, divination, and occultic practices

I bind the spirit Jezebel and Ahab

I bind the demon spirit leviathan and marine spirits

I bind the spirit basilisk (death and destruction)

I bind the spirit rejection

I bind the spirit mammon and greed

I bind the spirit lust

I bind spirit a broken heart

I bind the spirit pity and low self esteem

I bind the spirit self- hatred

I bind the spirit python and serpentine spirits

I bind the spirit sexual abuse (molestation, rape and torture)

I bind the spirit emotional abuse

I bind the spirit emotional abuse

I bind emotional rejection

I bind the spirit gang rape

I bind the spirit molestation

I bind the addictive spirit (sex, and drugs)

I bind the demon cyber-sex

I bind the spirits prostitution, harlotry, and whoredom

I bind the spirit of abandonment in the bloodline

I bind the spirit of parental neglect

I bind the spirit of physical/psychological and emotional abuse

I cast out every spirit that is named out by the roots and command you to walk in dry places until your day of destruction in the name of Jesus.

My Father, you arise and let every enemy be scattered of men today in the name of Jesus. I render Satan helpless and powerless before the blood of Jesus, in the name of Jesus.

I command every spirit that is not the Holy Spirit to depart now. I bind dark powers, principalities and territorial demons over communities in the name of Jesus.

In the name of Jesus, I call forth the warring angels to battle in the heavenlies against all powers of the enemy in Jesus name. I break the power of death and destruction by the blood of Jesus.

Father God I bind the spirit of pressure which keeps anger in the body set to damage men's health. I paralyze its powers and destroy it by the blood of Jesus, in Jesus name.

Father God teach men how to deal with their emotions it is not be put away and hidden my father but to be expressed to bring forth healing of the body in the name of Jesus. My father men do not wrestle against flesh and blood but against principalities rules and spiritual wickedness in heavenly places. In the name of Jesus, teach men to remain calm, in the times of injustice. Father God, give men clear vision to know anger is a weapon of the enemy sent to destroy their lives in Jesus name.

In the name of Jesus help, men make wise choices to be kind to others and forgiving others. Kind hearted forgiving one another and not envying each other in the name of Jesus. (Ephesians 4:26). My father your word says a soft answer turns away wrath, but a harsh word stirs up anger (Proverbs15:1).

Teach men daily to overlook and release situations that was sent to derail them from their purpose in Jesus name. Give men the mind and the willingness to take responsibility and accountability in the name of Jesus. In the name of Jesus, let men keep their purposes and dreams steadfastly before them in Jesus name. (Proverbs 15: 7-24)

I cover my family, my neighbors, my community, my state, my nation with the blood of Jesus. Father God 1 claim and secure your promise according Psalms 91; Isiah 74:17 and Exodus 12:13 as protection and shield in the name of Jesus. In the name of Jesus. I command a new brain, a new heart; anew mind in ___ from this day forth in Jesus name.

Father God, rain down your blessing upon men, salvation, healing, strength for the journey in the name of Jesus. As they take, one-step ahead open doors of opportunities to them in Jesus name. Bless our men indeed and enlarge their territory in Jesus name.

I declare and decree your blessing, favor peace, and joy over our men in Jesus name. I decree righteousness over my life and the life of every man in the name of Jesus. Father God 1 decree hope and a future for African American men in the name of Jesus. I declare and decree a hope and future for every man with a heart and desire to trust God for change in the name of Jesus. (Job 22:28) 1 seal this prayer by the blood of Jesus, in the name of Jesus. (Amen).

> And the fruit of righteousness is sown in peace of them that make peace. (James 3:18)

Prayer against Unrepentant Enemies

Father God in the name of Jesus, I soak myself in the blood of Jesus from the top of my head to the soles of my feet. My father I plead the blood of Jesus over my life, my possession and my family in the name of Jesus.

Let the blood of Jesus paralyze and dismantle every confederacy of the enemy in the name of Jesus operating in secret, operating in hiding against my life and those closely connected to me in Jesus name.

Father God destroys the mask of the enemy in the name of Jesus. In the name of Jesus, expose and disgrace opportunists and manipulators in my life in the name of Jesus.

My father every unfriendly friend walking close to me pretending friendship and masking deceit, destroy and expose the mask in the name of Jesus. My father open my eyes as you opened the eyes of Elijah's servant in the name of Jesus name.

Holy Spirit set my life on fire to see and discern people, places and things in the name of Jesus.

My father let signs and wonders be my lot in the mighty name of Jesus

Holy ghost power let the words from my mouth spoken in faith be a hammer in the camp of the enemy destroying, cancelling and paralyzing the works of the devils and his demons, witchcraft, sorcery, and divination in Jesus name.

Angels of war with flaming swords of fire move into the 2nd heaven and destroy with chaos, confusion, mayhem the plot and interference and sabotage of destructive and wicked spirits in the name of Jesus.

Let double destruction desecrate the territorial demons operating in high places over my family, my life my region, city, state and country in the name of Jesus.

Generational curses from my mothers and fathers side moving and destroying my future be destroyed by the blood of Jesus in Jesus name.

Spirit of frustration, division and separation be destroyed by fire in the name of Jesus.

In the name of Jesus I bind the spirit of lies/spirits of jealousy spirit of slumber.

My father let the word of God fire missiles of destruction and burn to ashes every secret confederacy of the enemy mitigating against my life and the life of my family in the name of Jesus.

Father God in the name of Jesus, paralyze spirits of false witness against my life and family in the name of Jesus.

Cancel and destroy the lying spirits in Jesus name

As Samuel hacked king Agag to pieces, let the sword of God wield destruction into the camp of witchcraft, sorcery, divination, enchanters, false prophets and agents of Satan with doctrines of lies in Jesus name. I bind the spirit of darkness and powers of wickedness in the 2nd heaven in the name of Jesus.

Let the enemies against my success, be struck with blindness and madness in the name of Jesus. (Deuteronomy 28:2)

Let the enemies against my prosperity and wealth be terrorized with astonishment in the name of Jesus. (Deuteronomy 28:28)

Father God in the name of Jesus, send cursing, vexation, pestilence, consumption into the heart of every agent of Satan used to bring sadness into my life and family in the name of Jesus. (Deuteronomy 28:22)

My father makes the heaven bronze above the heads of all my unrepentant enemies in the name of Jesus. (Deuteronomy 28:23)

My father make the earth iron under the feet of my unrepentant enemies in the name of Jesus. (Deuteronomy 28:23)

My generation shall inherit the blessings of God in Jesus name. Thank you my God for restoring the years of virtue, goodness, joy and peace that was stolen from my life. My Lord in the name of Jesus restore 100 folds and increase in my generations in the name of Jesus. You will restore what the locus, cankerworm and palmerworms has stolen in Jesus name (Joel 2: 25-26)

My father my life and the life of my family will demonstrate the blessings and favor of the Lord in the name of Jesus.

Thank you father God for destroying and cancelling the works of my unrepentant enemies over my life and the life of my family in the name of Jesus.

Thank you for the blessings of Deuteronomy 28:1-14 over my life and the life of my family, in blessings you will bless. My father what you have blessed no man can curse therefore I declare the blessings of the Lord makes rich and he adds no sorrow in Jesus name.

Thank you my father that my family is restored, set fee and healed in Jesus name. (Amen)

Deuteronomy 28:1-14, Deuteronomy 28:15-35, Genesis 14:20, Matthew 5:44. John 14:1, Luke 1:71, Psalms 91:15, Psalms18:17, Romans 12:1, Hebrews 10:36, 2 Thessalonians 5:17, Colossians 3:24

Prayer to release the Promise of God in Business/Career

Father God in the name of Jesus, I praise and honor you and glorify you as God.

Thank you Lord, I have a high priest who is touched by the feelings of my infirmities.

My father in the name of Jesus: I bind the spirit of lack, poverty, wastage, spirit of homelessness, vagabond spirit I release the promises of God in my business and life in the name of Jesus. I bind the spirit of the devourer in the name of Jesus (Malachi 3:11)

My father the blessings of the Lord makes rich and adds no sorrow (Prov. 10:22).

My father 1 are blessed going out and coming in 1 walk in the blessings according to the word of God in Jesus name. (Deuteronomy 28" 1-14)

My father as you called Isaac to go and plant in Gerar a barren country in the midst of a famine and he was able to show an increase of 100folds, Lord let me plant, water and reap 100-fold blessing in faith in Jesus name. "But thou shalt remember the LORD thy God: for *it is* he that giveth thee power to get wealth, that he may establish his covenant which he sware unto thy fathers, as *it is* this day. "(Deuteronomy 8:18)

Every man also to whom God hath given riches and wealth, and hath given him power to eat thereof, and to take his portion, and to rejoice in his labor; this *is* the gift of God. (Ecclesiastes 5:19)

1 thank you my father for the faith walk today and trust you to do a new thing in my life. You have restored my life and I declare and decree wealth and riches is in my career and business in the name of Jesus name. "Wealth and riches *shall be* in his house: and his righteousness endure forever". (Psalams112:3) (Amen).

Psalms 30:6, Deuteronomy 28: 1-14, Deuteronomy 8:18 Psalms 118:25, 2 Chronicles 1:2, Psalms 112:3, Phil 4:13, Proverbs 14:23. Proverbs 12:24. Eccelesties 9:10, Philippians 4:13

Marriage Mess-up Cleanup

My father give me the grace to clean up the mess I made in my marriage; I stand before you repenting of disobedience and rebellion in the name of Jesus.

Lord, forgive me of sexual sins; forgive me of adultery/ fornication. Forgive me for lusting after strange woman/strange man with the spirit of seduction and mystery. Lord, forgive me for touching the body of a man/woman that was not my spouse for that I ask you to forgive me in Jesus name.

My father, I am ashamed of my weakness, I ask you to give me strength to forsake the urging of my flesh to commit sin.

My father give me a clean heart and renew a right spirit within me.

My father God let me not cast away the confidence you have given me in marriage, it is great recompense to me through you my father, there are rewards in Jesus name (Hebrews 10:35)

Father God in the name of Jesus, destroy the allure of the strange woman/strange man sent against me to enslave me causing me to stray from my spouse in

Jesus name. My Lord, I ask you to cover my eyes with the blood of Jesus, so I will not desire the charms of the strange woman/strange man in Jesus name.

My father, let the blood of Jesus neutralize and paralyze the serpentine spirit of Jezebel sent to take my mind and seduce me into sexual sins in Jesus name.

Holy Spirit fire I bind and renounce every spirit of bewitchment, witchcraft and sorcery sent to control, manipulate, deceive and dominate my emotions in the name of Jesus.

Blood of Jesus no weapon that is formed against me shall proper in the name of Jesus.

I send the judgment of God against all evil doers' demon spirits sending destruction into my marriage in the name of Jesus.

Father God let the spirit of envy; jealousy and covetousness die a natural death in the name of Jesus.

I bind the spirit of bondage, spirit of double mindedness, spirit of pride, spirit of heaviness, spirit of jealousy in the name of Jesus.

Father God I send the judgment of death against every serpent and scorpion sent to destroy my home and family in the name of Jesus.

Let the power of the axe of God fall and cut off the head of every anti-marriage spirit bringing destruction to my marriage in Jesus name

In the name of Jesus as Elijah sent fire to destroy his enemies, my father send the fire of the Holy Spirit and the blood of Jesus and destroy every unrepentant enemy in the name of Jesus.

Every enemy mitigating against my marriage bring them into captivity, spoil the goods of the enemy by fire in Jesus name.

Father God devour my enemies let there be civil war in the 2nd heaven against every enemy of my marital success in the name of Jesus.

In the name of Jesus, close the door forever that was opened to a spirit wife or husband through disobedience or unholy covenants in Jesus name.

By the blood of Jesus I divorce the spirit husband and wife and turn my back on them forever in the name of Jesus.

In the name of Jesus destroy martial pictures documents, and marriage certificate in Jesus name.

Cancel the damage done to my natural marriage by the spirit husband or wife in Jesus name.

By the blood of Jesus uncover every secret sin hidden in my life and the life of my spouse in the name of Jesus.

I call forth divine healing over my marriage, I call forth joyful happy memories and a deep abiding love for my spouse in Jesus name.

Father God I plead the blood of Jesus over my marriage. My father bring all the good things you have in store for me in my marriage bring health and cure in Jesus name.

My father I declare and decree I shall have all the good things you have declared over my marriage today.

Father God show your great power in my marriage and bring forth divine restoration and supernatural healing in the Jesus name

Holy Spirit power let the miracles and transformation in my marriage be the catalyst to transform the lives of my family and my community in the name of Jesus.

My father I call forth peace joy and happiness in my marriage in the Jesus name.

I declare and decree my marriage is growing sweeter and sweeter each and every day in Jesus name.

In the name of Jesus, I call forth an all-consuming fire of love to envelop our hearts that we are knit together in the oneness of a covenant relationship. Let the bond of love remain firmly in place until death us do part in the name of Jesus.

My father what you joined together, let no demonic spirit, no principality or power, rulers of darkness put asunder in Jesus name (Amen).

1 John 1:19, John 20:23 1 Thessalonians 4: 3-5, 1 Corinthians 10:13, 1 Corinthians 6:18, 2 Timothy 2:22, Ephesians 5:22, James 5:16, Hebrews 4:16

Prayer for Career and Job release

Father God in the name of Jesus I bring our men before you today and thank you for increasing in their lives and careers, and businesses.

As you increase them my father stretch forth your hands into their lives, accelerate them to progressively increase daily thorough your fire in Jesus name.

My father in the name of Jesus I pray divine strategies over our men, supernatural moves of the Holy Spirit to catapult our men to the next level in their professions and careers in the name of Jesus.

I bind the spirit of witchcraft, sorcery and divination in the workplace in the name of Jesus.

I bind the spirit of lack and poverty in the name of Jesus'

I bind the spirit of wastage

I bind the spirit of homelessness the vagabond spirit in the name of Jesus

I bind the spirit of the devourer

I bind the spirit of idolatry

I come against the spirit of organizational glass ceilings, the spirits of racism and discrimination in Jesus name.

I come against the artificial gates in the name of Jesus. I come against managers withholding raises and promotions in the name of Jesus.

I come against department selectivity in the name of Jesus.

I come against the old boys network in the name of Jesus, 1 tear it down and destroy it to the root by the blood of Jesus.

I paralyze and destroy the spirit of cronyism in Jesus name.

I bind the elitist spirit in the name of Jesus.

I bind the spirit of witchcraft, divination and fortune telling in the workplace in the name of Jesus.

I bind the spirit of grudge and malice in the workplace in the name of Jesus.

I bind the spirit of Leviathan and marine in the name of Jesus.

I bind curses sent as spoken words in Jesus name.

I bind the trafficking demon in the name of Jesus.

I bind the demon spirit of office politics and internal harassment in Jesus name.

I bind the Jezebel and Ahab spirit in the name of Jesus.

I come against the spirit of bewitchment in the name of Jesus.

I come against the spirits of lust and perversion in Jesus name. 1 come against the spirit of sexual favors for promotions in Jesus name.

I bind the spirit of competition in the name of Jesus.

Father God as Elijah threw salt in the waters and the water became sweet, I declare sweet waters in the life of our men and their careers in the name of Jesus.

I bind and destroy opportunists, deceivers and manipulators in the workplace; demonic spirits sent to displace our men from their positions in Jesus name.

In the name of Jesus our men are rising, and growing to the glory of God. They are the head and never the tail, the top and not the bottom in Jesus name.

In the name of Jesus our men are blessed to prosper and succeed; what God has blessed no man can curse. (Amen and Amen)

Psalms 30:6, Deuteronomy 28: 1-14, Deuteronomy 8:18 Psalms 118:25, 2 Chronicles 1:2, Psalms 112:3

Colossians 3:23, Phil 4:13, Proverbs 14:23. Proverbs 12:24. Ecclesiastes 9:10, Philippians 4:13, Isiah 40:3

Peace I leave with you, my peace I give unto you: not as the world giveth, give I unto you. Let not your heart be troubled, neither let ii be afraid. (John 14:27)

Prayer against Backlash and Retaliation

My father I thank you that you are an amazing God. I thank you for divine protection through the blood of Jesus, in the name of Jesus Christ the son of God.

I hide now under the shadow of your wings according to Psalms 91 in Jesus name. "You are my Shepard, yea though I walk through the shadow of death I will fear no evil in the name of Jesus." (Psalms 23)

In the name of Jesus, I bind the spirits of backlash and retaliation and every spirit that was addressed during these prayers and decrees in the name of Jesus.

I bind any contact or attempts of reinforcement against my family, my possessions, or anyone connected to me in the name of Jesus. I destroy the power of the enemy by the blood of Jesus. I bind every co-hort spirit that will attempt to splinter, separate, alter or use other demonic means to control in Jesus name. I neutralize, cancel and destroy dominion, principalities, powers, rulers in high places now by the blood of Jesus, in the name of Jesus. You have no authority in my life or family in Jesus name. I command every spirit other than the Holy Spirit to depart to the pit of hell never return to disturb me, my family, my possessions, my community, my city, my state my nation in the name of Jesus. Your power is broken over this region and I command you by the blood of Jesus to depart never to return in the Jesus name Christ the son of God. (Amen)

Thank you my father for the many testimonies that will come forth through the prayers of faith in the name of Jesus.

I believe by faith the Lord answered prayers today and the manifestation of his power in the lives of families is seen in Jesus name. I know God met you at the point of your need and brought forth a mighty deliverance in your relationship and marriage.

Pray in faith, proclaim the word of God. Read the word of God, draw close to God and he will draw close to you.

Getting a breakthrough and keeping the breakthrough is a matter of consecration and right living. What God has destroyed in your life sinful life, do not go back and try to resurrect what was destroyed. Let the dead bury their dead, walk in the new life. Blessing I will bless you in Jesus name. (Amen).

Supplementary

Financial Problems/ Cursed Money:

Repent and ask for forgiveness. Begin to pay tithe and offering to the Lord. Malachi 3; 8-9 – 12, Luke 12; 16-21, James 5: 1-6, Proverbs 1:32, Jeremiah 12: 1-14, Psalms 73:3, Job 15:21, Jeremiah 12

Blessings – Prosperity

Malachi 3:10- 12, Joshua 1:8, 1 chronicles 22:13, Genesis26:12, Matthew 6:31-33, Deuteronomy 8:18, Deuteronomy 6: 10-13, Deuteronomy 24:19, Deuteronomy 30:8-10, Deuteronomy 28: 1-15

Parental Curse (Mother and Father):

Micah 7:6, Exodus 21:15, Matthew 15:4, Mark 7:10, Leviticus 20:9, Proverbs 6:20, Proverbs 1:8

Incest/illegitimacy – Deuteronomy 23:2, Leviticus 10:10, 1 Timothy 1:9, Leviticus 5:3,

Curse of Cain (Murder) Gen 4:8, Genesis 4:6, and Jude 1:11, Proverbs 3:33

Curse of Jezebel and Ahab 2 King 9:37, 1 Kings 21:23, Galatians 3:13, 22 Kings 9:11, 1 Kings 21:25, Deuteronomy 11:26, 22 Kings 9:7

Seeking physicians before seeking God, Acts 13:11, Mark 5:26, 11 Chronicles 16:12, Luke 8:43

Curse of Rebellion Deuteronomy 31:27, 1 Samuel 15:23, Proverbs 17:11, Jeremiah 28:16

Curse of Unbelief: EXODUS 10:9, Roman 3:3, Romans 11:20, Hebrews 3:12, Hebrews 4:11, 1 Timothy 1:3,

Curse of burning incense before other Gods

(Smoking etc.) -11 Chronicles 26:17, Psalms 18:18. I Corinthians 6:12, I Corinthian 3:17, James 4:17

Curse of infirmity (Sickness and Disease)

Leviticus 12:2, Luke 13:11, John 5:5, Mark 6:7, Ephesian 6:12 II Corinthians 10:3-4)

ABOUT THE AUTHOR

Marcia Meikle-Naughton is a woman that walked a pathway overrun with ravines, trenches, and sinkholes. From an emotional perspective each mile helped to shape Marcia into the woman of God she is today in focus, attitude, relationships and purpose. Marcia had to trust God and allowed the loving presence of the Holy Spirit to touch her heart and aid her in releasing hurtful memories. She experienced life events that would have crippled and stifled the creative person she is today; however, the Holy Spirit shielded her heart and kept her soft and pliable in the hands of the Lord and Savior Jesus Christ.

Marcia came to the United States as an Immigrant from Jamaica West Indies. She was educated in the American School system from middle school to graduate school, adapting a culture very dissimilar than her own. Raised by strict Jamaican parents, Marcia spent most of her private times reading books as a little girl with a very vivid imagination. Marcia tried to live the life she read about and sought out love and found disappointment and heart break instead.

Over the years revolving relationships and engagements, after broken engagement #3, Marcia experienced a life changing transition, graduation with a Master's degree in Business and 3 months pregnant.

The birth of her daughter Brianna gave Marcia purpose and a plan for the future. Deep diving into a Wall Street career Marcia grew in the company and branched off to start her own business. Marcia learned in the process that God is the keeper and sustainer of life, Jesus was the anchor that kept her going year after year.

Through the love of Jesus Marcia learned how to forgive people and release them in her heart and mind. Marcia came to the realization and revelation the power of forgiveness in bringing transformation in her life and those connected to her. In the release God unleased blessings in every area and aspect of her life. Latent gifts and talents suddenly were visible. She started believing God for the impossible and began walking in faith doing what she was not willing and reluctant to attempt. Obedience opened a floodgate of blessings: ventures tried began bearing fruit in great abundance. Forgiving people and lastly forgiving herself unlocked a flow gate of blessings – total release of people and most importantly forgiving herself and accepting herself with rights and responsibilities as a human being, who is not perfect.

Marcia is a woman of God, wife and mother. Marcia is also a successful reggae and gospel music recording artist, under the artist name Lady Peace MN. Her first solo single" Story Book Children, and subsequent releases in 2015 with an upcoming CD release in 2016, "Music from the Heart", is a testimony of the transforming power of the Lord and Savior Jesus Christ. Marcia is a published author and writer of short stories and mini screenplays and videos.

Marcia holds an MBA in Business and is a Project Manager/Program Manager. Marcia is an entrepreneur building businesses one by one! According to the word of God, if you can imagine it God can do so much more (my paraphrase). The Spa/ beauty and makeup business is her passion away from music and the creative arts; Marcia has great boulder like dreams and visions. The Holy Spirit provides direction and guidance and fuel her imagination and dreams to higher heights of accomplishments, in the name of Jesus."

Marcia Meikle- Naughton (Aka: Lady Peace MN)